DREAMSCAPES

DREAMSCAPES

Inspiration and beauty in gardens near and far

CLAIRE TAKACS

hardie grant books

CONTENTS

CLOUDEHILL

OLINDA, VICTORIA

Cloudehill, the garden of Jeremy and Valerie Francis, is one that is very close to my heart. It was the first garden I ever photographed in 2006 and it became the inspiration for my career. I'd already been experimenting with landscape photography, my initial love, and had started getting up at dawn to see the natural world cast in a different light.

One of my projects while I was studying photography brought me to Cloudehill. When walking around the garden for the first time, I was immediately struck by its beauty. Previously I had only seen such gardens in England, so it was a surprise to find this ten minutes from where I'd grown up. I was also struck by the ephemeral nature of this beauty and an almost urgent sense that no-one was here capturing it. So, I met and chatted with Jeremy, creator of this magnificent garden, and organised to come back and photograph it. The next morning, after having jumped the fence at 5am, it was a revelation to me to be lost in the beauty of this garden, then to observe the light as it gradually came through and illuminated its different parts. My eyes went to wherever the light was and I started to appreciate the garden's many colours, textures, layers and design elements. I was incredibly inspired and compelled to capture and record all I saw. My love of light seemed to facilitate both seeing and capturing the beauty of the garden and it's been the key element that has guided my work ever since.

Jeremy and Valerie initially lived on a wheat and sheep farm in hot, dry Western Australia. During regular trips to England, Valerie's homeland, Jeremy became inspired by the plants and gardens he saw there, particularly the Arts and Crafts masterpieces, such as Sissinghurst and Hidcote, and the works of Gertrude Jekyll.

It was during this time he realised the effect
a garden could have on someone. He vividly
describes how he was affected by the element
of 'expectation and surprise'—a phrase coined
by Long Barn's Harold Nicolson—particularly
the experience of Hidcote, with its cross axis
opening that reveals a staggering view of the
surrounding countryside. Jeremy has gone on
to use it to great effect in Cloudehill's many
garden rooms.

In 1988, Jeremy began collecting his wishlist
of perennials, unavailable in Australia, from
a number of influential English nurseries and
plantspeople, including Christopher Lloyd
(page 178) and Beth Chatto. Of the 140
perennials he brought back with him, 120 were
eventually released after passing quarantine. A
change of direction a few years later provided
an opportunity to seek out a more suitable

environment to grow the cool-climate perennials to which he was drawn, and experiment with garden design. David Glenn from Lambley (page 62), who had been given some of the initial collection, suggested the Dandenongs, an hour from Melbourne, as the ideal place. In 1991, after years of searching, he found Cloudehill, a former nursery and flower farm owned by Jim Woolrich.

The inspiration provided by this internationally influenced garden really was the beginning for me and set me on a road I'm still travelling—one that takes me around the globe seeking and sharing beauty and inspiration in the world's gardens. It's been an incredible focus for my life and has brought about so many connections to wonderful people in the gardening world. Cloudehill connected me to Australian writer Christine Reid, and subsequently became my first of many features in *Gardens Illustrated*, which has also been central to my work.

In the intervening years, I've returned to Cloudehill many times and become friends with Jeremy. It's always nice to see the garden's development, and the seasonal changes are stunning. The perennial borders are at their best in late summer, when the colours and textures lead the eye to a view of a eucalypt stand in the distance. In winter, you can really appreciate the structure of the garden and its many rooms, while in spring, the garden comes alive with meadows of bluebells.

MOUNT MACEDON GARDEN

MOUNT MACEDON, VICTORIA

Michael McCoy is one of Australia's most talented and plant-driven garden designers and he's teamed with very hands-on owners to create a stunning perennial garden in Victoria's Macedon Ranges.

Although the garden is almost completely planted with exotic species, plants have been selected that grow in similar environmental conditions, which is a great example of the notion that plant performance is perhaps more important than geographical origin. Here, in this garden, plants seem to be in harmony with each other and the setting.

To me, this garden has an almost dream-like quality through beautiful use of colour. Clumping of species with occasional emergents and the self-seeding of species such as *Verbascum* and *Digitalis* is used to great effect. Sweeps of key species are repeated throughout the space, deliberately bouncing left and right of the network of gravel paths, so that when any particular species is in bloom, it echoes around you and into the distance. This results in a real overall unity, but manages to avoid any monotony as there is a constant, subtle shift in the mix of plants at all times.

I enjoyed spending a bit of time with Michael in the garden in the evening, both with our cameras and waiting for the clouds to pass and backlight the golden *Stipa gigantea*. I loved the combination of this with the blue agapanthus.

I photographed mid-February, at the end of a hot Australian summer, so it's amazing to see a garden thriving and with so much colour in this harsh environment. The light was perfect for photography, both in the evening and then again at sunrise, with just a hint of mist as the light began appearing through the trees bordering the garden.

The surrounding trees create a beautiful sense of enclosure for the garden, and I love the loosely framed but subtle views through the perennials and informal gravel paths out to the distant landscape. This was also a stunning garden viewed from above. Standing on a ladder at sunrise, I could appreciate the absolute beauty of this design.

SALLY JOHANNSOHN GARDEN

NIEKA, TASMANIA

The garden of Sally Johannsohn and her husband, writer Andrew Darby, on the side of Mount Wellington is one of my favourite gardens in Australia. It's hard to believe she is only fifteen minutes outside the Tasmanian capital of Hobart, as the garden feels like a world unto itself. It has an enviable setting, with views across one side of the mountain towards the distant D'Entrecasteaux Channel and a stunning lake with a backdrop of eucalyptus at another end. It is Sally's hugely creative and clever planting with interesting plants, however, that really makes this garden stand out.

Sally is a plant hunter and has imported many exotic species, which she grows for her onsite nursery, also called Plant Hunters. Here she specialises in unusual cool-climate perennials from Asia, the North American woodlands and Europe.

Every year Sally travels to another region of the world, exploring and spending time learning and working in great gardens, such as Chanticleer in Philadelphia. She also spends time hunting and observing plants in the wild. Sally is inspired by the planting she sees internationally with the New Perennial movement, but in her own garden she experiments with plants different from those normally used in such a style. Her garden seems to have really settled and is thriving with this more naturalistic style of planting. I admire that Sally is incredibly generous with the knowledge she has accrued and you can now see her influence trickling down into other Tasmanian gardens.

Sally draws on her training as a florist to incorporate colours and textures in the plantings. Another major feature is her repeated use of curves throughout the garden, including in stone walls and benches. This reflects the amphitheatre nature of the mountains and valleys surrounding the property. She also mows her lawn to reflect the contours of the land, each year experimenting with slightly different shapes.

Sally's garden is incredibly seasonal, with interest continuing throughout the year. I particularly loved photographing this garden in the mist. I felt the conditions perfectly suited the magic of this great garden.

FIRE AND BEAUTY

YALLINGUP,
WESTERN AUSTRALIA

With its outlook to the untouched landscape of the Leeuwin-Naturaliste National Park and Smiths Beach, this garden has some of the most enviable views I've seen in Australia. The owner, Bill Mitchell, used to work in finance and has no formal training as a gardener. Nor did he hire anyone to help him five years ago when it came to designing what has become a much-admired garden. In fact, Bill used to surf a lot, but this Mexican-themed garden he and his wife Di have called Fire and Beauty, has now taken over as his passion.

This area, called Yallingup, near the Margaret River region in Western Australia, is considered to be at a high risk from bushfires, so when they moved in Bill and Di cleared much of the dry and dangerous native vegetation that surrounded their home. Their idea was to create a garden

that was fire retardant and would help protect their home. Bill has used both Australian natives and exotics, including thousands of succulents, cacti and aloes which, because of their high water content, don't catch on fire. They make up a 30-metre (100-foot) buffer around the house. Additional fire prevention measures include a water storage system so roof sprinklers can be operated.

In 2016, Bill won *Gardening Australia*'s Gardener of the Year competition in the large garden category. Not only does the garden serve a purpose, but there's plenty of interest and beauty here, too, with the different textures, colours, layers and mass plantings of species. With more than twenty aloe varieties, Bill and Di are thought to have one of the largest private collections in Australia.

BANONGIL

SKIPTON, VICTORIA

I've never seen a display of daffodils like this anywhere in Australia. When spring arrives, it is just spectacular and looks like something you might find in England, although with a uniquely Australian backdrop of river red gums running alongside a creek. These daffodils have been making an appearance here for more than a century.

Banongil is a historic property located in Skipton, near Ballarat in Victoria's Western District, and the 5.5-hectare (13.6-acre) garden is part of a much larger station. You get some perspective of just how big it is when you arrive. There is a stunning driveway that winds for five kilometres (three miles) through beautiful countryside and past stands of gum trees to take you to the homestead on the hill. I particularly loved the part of this winding road where the red flowering gum (*Corymbia ficifolia*) had dropped its flowers in mass onto the drive.

This land was first settled back in the 1830s, but the gardens were thought to have been designed in part by William Guilfoyle, for the owner at the time, Charles Fairbairn. Guilfoyle was the landscape architect of Melbourne's Royal Botanic Gardens, in the early twentieth century. You can see Guilfoyle's signature

sweep of lawn that runs from the homestead all the way down to the river, as well as the use of Canary Island palm trees on that same lawn. Close to the homestead are more ordered gardens with gravel paths, formal rose beds and a croquet lawn. Wander further, however, and you'll discover the 'wild' gardens and their fruit trees. During spring, the lawns are left to grow while the daffodils and bluebells are flowering.

The day I went there with my camera was very special. Mist was coming off the dam and the early morning light was soft and perfect. I had visited the previous evening, as I always do if I can, to meet the garden owners, start to get to know the garden and also begin to photograph parts of it. I love to capture both directions of light, working during the hours either side of sunset and sunrise. I often find, though, that my morning shoots, when I am freshest, the garden is quiet and the light often the most atmospheric, are the most successful. At that time of day in this garden, the stone terraces built to show off the various types of daffodils bred by the Fairbairns back in the 1930s are bathed in sunshine. Over time, the cultivars have cross-pollinated and many are indistinguishable, but their display is as stunning as ever.

FROGMORE

LERDERDERG, VICTORIA

Owners Jack Marshall and Zena Bethell have been creating a very personal and exciting garden near Trentham, Victoria, experimenting with ideas and inspiration drawn from overseas. Frogmore is a completely plant-driven garden, envisaged as a space with long walks, bordered by hornbeam and English box punctuated by gardens with distinct styles and colours. The Formal Gardens are their version of Monet's 'paintboxes' where, each season, they experiment with colour themes. These twin borders are most spectacular at sunset—it's then you can appreciate their true painterly feel. The Prairie Garden is an interpretation of the New Wave planting evolving in Europe and the United States, yet to be fully embraced in Australia. Australia's harsh climate prevents growing many of the plants commonly used in the prairie planting style, so this is really an experiment to see what species will grow in these conditions and which plant communities will thrive.

STONEFIELDS

DAYLESFORD, VICTORIA

Paul Bangay is one of Australia's most high-profile garden designers and for more than twenty-five years has been creating gardens for prominent figures in business and culture, both in Australia and internationally. He is celebrated for his elegant approach, creating gardens of classic simplicity and symmetry, particularly with the use of hedging and topiary often in the form of *Buxus sempervirens* spheres and cubes.

Stonefields is Paul's home garden, near Daylesford in Victoria. I loved visiting this garden for the first time, with the challenge of photographing it for *Gardens Illustrated*. I captured many of the more obvious views that I'd seen of this much-photographed garden, but particularly loved this new view I hadn't seen of Paul's Red Garden. This image was taken from a ladder at sunset, where I could see the distant eucalyptus forest. When I took the photograph, it was a profusion of roses and clouds of cow parsley set against clipped box spheres.

On entry, there's a strong linear aspect to the garden, with stepped terraces leading down to the farmhouse. A rill—a narrow channel that carries water—leads the eye down the terraces and to the house. One of the garden rooms, the White Garden, was inspired by Vita

Sackville-West's English garden at Sissinghurst and has beds of white roses and irises, a central pool covered with waterlilies and a backdrop of pleached hornbeams.

Taking photographs of country gardens is generally my preference. I was originally inspired by landscape photography, and I love to show the connection between the garden and the wider landscape. My favourite gardens are those that transition to their surrounds subtly and with no distinct edges between garden and greater landscape.

Utilising the soft light at sunrise or sunset often enhances big landscape views. There was only a brief moment on the morning I visited with beautiful soft light, and I used it to capture Paul's long pool surrounded by lawn. This reflective pool leads the eye straight out to the surrounding landscape so simply and beautifully. I also enjoyed seeing his use of perennials, which has become freer and more naturalistic in style, in contrast to the clipped forms. This is a hugely ambitious and beautiful garden created in the relatively short timeframe of about ten years. It's an oasis carved from the surrounding bare paddocks and a testament to Paul's talent.

GOLDEN HILLS

GLENGARRY, TASMANIA

Jodi Broomby's garden, tucked away in Tasmania's Tamar Valley, really blew me away when, with Sally Johannsohn who introduced me, I first saw it on a hot summer's day in 2016. It's such a brilliant combination when an avid plant lover and grower combines this passion with her artistic side.

With Jodi's use of colour and inspiring planting combinations, her garden, which wraps around her house and adjacent nursery—also called Golden Hills—exudes energy and creativity. She explained that when she saw influential Dutch garden designer Piet Oudolf's work 'she was in love'. Jodi has taken the naturalistic style of gardening championed by Oudolf, a leading figure of the New Perennial movement, and run with it in her own unique way. I have seen many gardens with this feel and style internationally, but very few in Australia, which is why it's wonderful to see Jodi experimenting with and interpreting these ideas and creating a garden that feels a little wilder and closer to nature here. In any pocket of the garden, you'll find a mix of herbs, grasses and flowers, from roses to rare perennials, as well as drought-resistant varieties, built up in layers from smaller plants to larger shrubs. I hope we see more of this style of planting in Australia in future.

It's a garden of great passion and you can feel this when you're there. My favourite part of the garden this visit was at the front, where a narrow path leads through a stunning planting combination that was backlit by the setting sun to highlight *Nepeta* 'Six Hills Giant', *Macleaya cordata*, *Echinops bannaticus*, *Achillea millefolium* 'Cerise Queen' and *Anthemis tinctoria* 'Kelwayi Yellow'.

This garden is just a small part of a much larger property, Jodi's family's dairy farm. When she's not milking the cows, she is in the beds or in the propagation tunnel where she raises dozens of seedlings and cuttings to sell through her specialist nursery, which offers a large range of perennials to Tasmanian gardeners.

PHILLIP JOHNSON GARDEN

OLINDA, VICTORIA

For more than twenty years, Phillip Johnson has been hugely successful in creating inspiring, productive and sustainable landscapes that not only address the demands of increasing water restrictions and climatic changes, but also celebrate and echo Australia's natural beauty.

Through his use of native plants, Phillip's gardens have a distinct link to the Australian bush, even in the suburbs. In 2013, Phillip Johnson Landscapes won Best in Show at the prestigious Chelsea Flower Show, a lifetime goal of Phillip's and a first for Australia.

This is his own garden at Olinda in Victoria's Dandenong Ranges, about an hour's drive from Melbourne. The region is known for its temperate rainforest and this garden is an example of how Phil's work sits so seamlessly within the native landscape. Apart from its obvious beauty, it is also a habitat for native animals, including lyrebirds, wombats, king parrots, echidnas and frogs.

Having once been a rock climber, Phillip has a strong understanding of formations and his placement of rocks in all of his gardens is incredibly natural. He also creates waterfalls, natural, chemical-free swimming pools and ponds in many of the gardens he designs. The waterfalls here at Olinda are stunning as they become illuminated by the early morning light rising up over the mountain. The ponds fill up naturally when it rains, and are fed at other times by a recycling and storage system. Phillip describes them as billabongs, an Australian term normally used to describe an isolated pond left behind after a river changes course. In his own garden, he has a natural swimming pool, complete with hot tub, surrounded by towering mountain ash trees and mature tree ferns. Below it, on the steep property there's another billabong that is home to a school of silver perch.

HILLANDALE

YETHOLME, NEW SOUTH WALES

Located in Yetholme, one of the coldest regions in Australia at around 1150 metres (3770 feet) above sea level, and an hour's drive from the Blue Mountains near Sydney, lies an inspiring garden, created by owners Sarah and Andrew Ryan. In 1999, they purchased the property from the Wilmott family who were responsible for planting most of the mature trees that provide a beautiful atmosphere and maturity to the space. Since taking ownership, Sarah and Andrew have been sensitively rejuvenating the garden, hoping to retain the original gardener's vision, while adding new areas and expanding and evolving the planting. Sarah, a passionate plantswoman, has cast her wonderfully artistic eye over this 2.5-hectare (6-acre) garden, part of the couple's 70-hectare (175-acre) property.

The garden consists of several areas, including a vegetable garden, cut flower bed, glasshouse and shaded glen with native ferns, rhododendrons, azaleas, hydrangeas and maples. From here a narrow, beautifully shaped, spring-fed water rill winds down to a lake where the

garden opens up and feels like an English landscape garden.

In 2003, on the sunny northern side of the garden, Sarah and Andrew created a dreamy herbaceous perennial border. It's 120 metres (390 feet) long and designed to be walked through, 'so as to immerse oneself in the planting, hopefully awakening and delighting the senses'. Sarah has never travelled outside New South Wales, but became interested in perennials about twenty years ago, influenced by the naturalistic planting style pioneered by the Dutch and spectacular herbaceous borders prevalent in the British Isles. The borders are experimental, and a lot has been learned over the years as Sarah's gained experience. She's used more than 300 different species to create 'movement, structure, texture and drama', and also plants to attract birds and insects into the garden. The border peaks at the end of summer and continues through into autumn. This is a garden I want to continue visiting, and one I hope will inspire many other gardeners.

STRINGYBARK COTTAGE

NOOSA, SUNSHINE COAST, QUEENSLAND

Just a short drive from the stunning beaches of Noosa, on Queensland's Sunshine Coast, garden designer Cheryl Boyd has created a unique and very personal garden during the past twenty-five years. It's a lush garden that sits beautifully within a towering native eucalyptus forest. I loved seeing the cleverly designed mass plantings of subtropical to cool-climate species, as Cheryl has favoured foliage texture, form and colour over flowers.

There are so many layers at work here from the groundcover up. Tall tree ferns shade bromeliads, while epiphytes hang in the forks of crepe myrtles and orchids are nestled among old tree trunks. From the shaded back veranda of the house the openness of the lawn creates a space to pause before you enter the more densely planted areas of the garden.

Cheryl is also recognised for her beautifully placed and subtle use of sculpture, much of which she creates herself. Her sculptures are scattered throughout the garden and its various rooms. As you enter the drive you are greeted with sculptures in the shape of teepees crafted from twigs, and two-metre-wide installations suspended above the ground.

One of Cheryl's favourite places in the garden is beside the fire pit beneath towering red stringybarks; from one of their branches another sculpture—this one made from leftover barbed wire—hangs high. At the end of the day, Cheryl loves to light a fire here and sit with a glass of wine and savour the soft evening light.

LAMBLEY

In the middle of Victoria's Goldfields region lies one of Australia's most inspiring and loved gardens, Lambley. David Glenn, who moved to Australia from the UK about a quarter of a century ago, is most noted for working with the excessive drought conditions that endured here for more than twelve years to create a garden that is full of colour and interest throughout the year. He has become one of this country's greatest proponents of dry-climate gardening, providing only supplementary watering to his garden three to four times a year.

His and wife Criss Canning's Lambley Nursey and Gardens is located in Ascot, just outside of Ballarat, and the climate is harsh. During winter the temperatures drop below freezing; in summer, they can top 40 °C (104 °F). With the frost and often incredibly dry conditions, it's hard to believe David and Criss could achieve such a vibrant and interesting garden.

Although Australia has many drought-resistant native species, David has looked further afield and selected plants from other dry regions in the world—including the Mediterranean, Central Asia, Chile, Mexico, Morocco, California, South Africa and the Canary Islands. He believes you should choose plants to suit the climate, rather than manipulate the environment to suit the garden. As an artist, however, it is Criss who has helped immensely with the design of the spaces and the colour combinations.

I love sunset in the Dry Garden. It's at this time of day you can really appreciate the many different textures, colours and layers of planting. The newer Mediterranean Garden is also an exciting addition, planted in the past four years. While I was there, the *Salvia sclarea* 'Archibalds Form', collected in Turkey more than thirty years ago, was in flower.

Lambley has many seasonal highlights, but perhaps one of the dreamiest occurs in autumn, when the pathway lined with *Salvia azurea* (azure blue sage) in the Ornamental Garden is backlit at sunrise.

WYCHWOOD

MOLE CREEK, TASMANIA

Located about 40 kilometres (25 miles) from Devonport in Tasmania, is Wychwood, one of Tasmania's most loved gardens. Its previous owners, Karen Hall and Peter Cooper, created a small paradise for themselves in their one-hectare (2.5-acre) garden during a period of twenty years and it is now being enjoyed and evolved by David Doukidis and Matt Bendall, two young and ambitious gardeners from Melbourne.

One of the garden's most interesting features is its famous labyrinth. Look around, though, and you'll see those curvaceous forms mirrored in other aspects: lawns that curve into borders filled with perennial plantings, the garden's carefully clipped hedges, and narrow paths that follow the contours of the landscape.

While it's beautiful all year around—spring is a riot of colour, while winter often brings a dusting of snow to the hedges and trees—I visited in autumn. The rich golds and deep reds of the changing maple leaves are as visually appealing as the pink of the *Sedum* 'Autumn Joy' that flowers through until the end of the season and the tall *Miscanthus* with its sweeping heads of flowers and seeds. There is also a small orchard where heritage apple trees are heavy with fruit at this time of year.

One of my favourite scenes is the simplicity but absolute beauty of the narrow winding path carved into the lawn that winds past two Adirondack chairs, then the clipped shapes of the English box with a cypress in the distance.

When you're deep in this garden it's almost as if you're cut off from the rest of the world, unless you look closely. There are glimpses of the farmland and working sheds that lie just beyond the boundary. I'm so glad the story of Wychwood will continue with its new owners and that it remains a garden that can be admired and enjoyed by visitors during its weekly openings.

RIDGEFIELD

COLDSTREAM, VICTORIA

Robert Boyle is one of Victoria's most-renowned landscape designers and he has worked tirelessly in the industry for more than forty years, creating inspiring gardens. His most famous garden is a collaboration with Di Johnson at the Garden Vineyard, one of the eighty gardens profiled in Monty Don's *Around the World in 80 Gardens* series for the BBC.

Here, at Ridgefield, Robert has created a garden of great beauty that perfectly suits the personalities of owners Paulette and Warwick Bisley. The first stage of the Coldstream garden in Victoria's Yarra Valley was completed in 1999, after Robert had collaborated with architect John Pizzey, who was designing the couple's mudbrick home.

Paulette's passion is roses and there are more than 450 varieties on show, from tea roses to Australian-bred climbing varieties. I loved the arch covered in clematis and roses where the washing hangs beneath.

I also love the way Robert's strong design and characteristic clipping of westringia is then softened by mass plantings of flowers including lavender, roses and clematis. The Bisleys' desire to protect themselves from winds but maintain their views out to the rolling hills of the Yarra Valley has worked beautifully. One of my favourite images taken on the misty morning I was there is the scene of red roses in the garden framing the view to the cows grazing in the distance. It's a beautiful garden, so well designed by Robert and loved by its passionate owners.

PEAR TREE WALK

LALLA, TASMANIA

The first time I visited this garden near Lalla, in Tasmania's northeast, it was autumn and, although the English-style landscape garden can be enjoyed at any time of year, I knew I'd have to return. This garden is called Pear Walk because of a lane of trees planted at the beginning of the twentieth century. During spring, it becomes a spectacular tunnel of blossoms with azaleas, rhododendrons and forget-me-nots lining the walk.

Rhonnie and Bob Pammenter were first attracted to the property by an avenue of sequoias from the front gate. Later, when they were clearing overgrown paddocks, they discovered the arch of pears. It wasn't the only hidden garden on the property. They also found an arbour completely overgrown by blackberries. Now, what they refer to as the Wild Walk winds below rhododendrons and deciduous trees, ending at a flowering tulip tree thought to be the oldest in Tasmania.

But the Pammenters also continued to develop the garden, planting new trees to create walkways through it. It's a garden concerned with beauty in an idyllic setting and, among the rolling hills of the Tasmanian countryside, it sits beautifully within the landscape.

FISHERMANS BAY

AKAROA, SOUTH ISLAND

Jill and Richard Simpson's garden on the
remote Banks Peninsula on New Zealand's
South Island is one I have come to love very
much, even though I have only visited once. I am
so glad for Instagram, so that I can keep an eye
on its evolution.

Gardens Illustrated published a feature with
these pictures and text by Australian writer
Christine Reid. I love Jill's philosophy and her
explanation of it to Christine: 'It took gardening
in such a visually dominant environment to
make me realise how completely a garden is
of its own place.' The wider landscape and the
changing light will always have the greatest
influence and Jill always considers them when
she plants, so that each element she introduces
links back to nature.

Even though the Simpsons moved here in the
late 1990s, they only turned their undivided
attention from the farm to the garden ten years
ago. The initial inspiration was conservation,
and their farm includes a hundred hectares
(250 acres) of regenerating native bushland.
However, more recently the garden has come to
be their sole creative outlet and each part of it
represents a different time in their lives. Most
recently Jill has been influenced by Europe's
New Perennial movement and the prairie
gardens of the United States. She has whole-
heartedly taken on the challenge to interpret
this to suit the raw beauty and local conditions
of the New Zealand landscape.

BLAIR

When Janet and John Blair found their stone cottage more than four decades ago, it was surrounded by farmland and backed by a stunning view of the snow-capped Remarkables mountain range, just outside of Queenstown. It was, however, built on an extremely exposed site, prone to icy winds. Janet began to plant trees for protection and shade, and has been working on the garden ever since, surrounding herself with beauty and planting everything you can see on the 6-hectare (15-acre) site.

Often, while I'm visiting gardens around the world, it enters my mind that these places are actually works of art, and that's never been truer than when I photographed here. Janet came back to me and said that my photographs were taken as though I was sitting on her shoulders. It's a garden I really connected to and I admire Janet so much for her passion and hard work, crafting and maintaining this most beautiful of gardens.

When I arrived, the curved drive was a tunnel of golden ash trees and horse chestnuts, and the house sat so gently within the landscape. The intimate garden behind the house, with its clipped box set against old apricot trees, wisteria and ornamental grapevine, was particularly special in autumn with vivid shades of yellow, red and green. There's no parking for cars beside the house—instead they are tucked away out of sight in a rustic shed covered in vegetation.

The garden is composed of many walks, often romantic in feel. My favourite was one that had the white berries of *Sorbus cashmiriana* on one side and multicoloured *Cornus* on the other. Janet has also used hedges—box, beech and hornbeam—throughout the garden. Sometimes they are clipped into whimsical topiaries or a serpentine hedge; other times they lead the eye (and walkers) to a gate in the distance or along a path to the vegetable garden, the first addition to the property when the Blairs moved in.

I was determined to capture this garden in good light and, on my fourth attempt over a number of days, I finally got what I needed to document this spectacular scene. I climbed the mown grass pathways up the northern slope behind the house where I could see every tree Janet had planted, as well as the dramatic mountainous backdrop, and there I waited until the light hit the foreground grasses at just the right moment.

QUEENSTOWN GARDEN

QUEENSTOWN, SOUTH ISLAND

Mountains and water are two elements I am hugely drawn to, so I had to go to New Zealand, particularly the South Island, to immerse myself in this breathtaking landscape and see what its gardens were like. I came across Brooke Mitchell from Baxter Design Group in Queenstown. This garden, located in the Wakatipu Basin of New Zealand's Otago region, has one of the most dramatic settings I have seen. Rather than compete with the extensive views or the architecturally designed home, he decided to let the landscape dictate the design of the garden.

The planting is fairly minimalistic, utilising only a small number of species, most of them native to New Zealand. Masses of native flaxes and grasses—including *Carex testacea* and *Libertia*, as well as low-growing shrubs, such as *Hebe*—are planted in a series of sweeping garden beds that directs your eye towards the landscape. A boardwalk reflects the form of the river below and mounds mimic the shapes of the distant mountains. In autumn, this region is shrouded in brilliant colour and the designers have used pin oaks, liquidambar and maple to mirror that seasonal colour and blend the garden with its surrounds.

LOS ALTOS

LOS ALTOS, CALIFORNIA

When Noel Kingsbury first introduced me to Brandon Tyson in 2009, I formed a connection and deep admiration for both the man and his work. The garden world is full of the most wonderful people and it's been a privilege to spend time in Brandon's world—I've revisited him and his gardens several times—and those he creates for his clients.

I can understand why he is one of northern California's most sought-after designers. Originally from Georgia, Brandon recently moved back there to create his own garden paradise filled with palm trees, but returns to California to work on select projects. He's a true designer, and I can't imagine his creativity, whatever form it takes, could ever cease.

This garden in Los Altos, on the San Francisco Peninsula, was a dream project for Brandon and, created over a period of just three years, is one of his greatest works. Like several of his projects, his clients on this one gave him an open brief and really let Brandon work his magic. Brandon said he pulled out all the stops with this one, bringing in rare and mature plants and trees from across the country. Brandon is known as a truly plant-driven designer who has a deep reverence for their diversity and unique personalities, as well as an amazing eye for unexpected pairings.

This garden surrounds a Mediterranean-style family home, and it's such a beautiful space to walk around, constantly changing as you move through the different plantings in each area. In parts, it can feel as though you're exploring a botanical garden. There is plenty of colour on show, one of the key design factors in this garden.

One of my favourite views is down a winding path bordered on each side by yellow *Santolina*. I also love the arbours Brandon has created from branches of oaks removed from the original garden. My other favourite view winds its way through 800 *Lavandula* x *intermedia* 'Provence', *Yucca rostrata* and Italian cypress (pencil pines). Brandon has used plants from all over the world in this garden, including some Australian natives, that thrive in the full sun, hot summers and mild winters. Plants have been selected for their bold geometric forms, and select specimen trees, such as the eighteen ancient olive trees, are displayed as works of art on mounds.

There are many seating areas throughout the garden, including a covered one just outside the family room of the home. It overlooks a huge fan palm, with clipped boxwood balls and succulents lining the adjoining terrace with its circular theme. Not surprisingly, the owners are thrilled with their garden, but as Brandon said, 'Just wait, it's only going to get better.'

WINDCLIFF

INDIANOLA, WASHINGTON

This is the very famous second home and garden of plantsman, author, plant collector and lecturer Dan Hinkley and his husband, Robert Jones. They purchased the property in Indianola, Washington, in 2000. At the time, they were still living at their nursery Heronswood (see page 138), but decided they wanted more privacy. Their move took them from a shaded woodland garden to a site of full sun, exposed to the wind on a cliff's edge. Still, it is one of the most beautiful settings I have seen for a garden.

Like Heronswood, Windcliff is home to an incredible collection of rare and unusual plants that Dan has collected from the wild. He's been on more than sixty-five trips to about twenty countries, and there are more than 2000 taxa (genera, species etc) growing in this botanical wonderland. Dan continues to travel, bringing attention to the immense diversity of the Earth's plant life.

The house, designed by Robert, sits gently within the 4.5-hectare (11-acre) property, where narrow paths wind around, taking in waterfalls, pools and rills, a bamboo grove and a circular fire pit with seating area. The back garden, overlooking Puget Sound, is a highly textural tapestry of colour and form. When I visited at the end of June, *Agapanthus campanulatus* from South Africa and *Lobelia tupa* from Chile were in flower; particularly stunning were the drooping plumes of New Zealand native *Austroderia fulvida* (toetoe) backlit by the morning sun.

This shoot was a case of right place, right time. I was with renowned Seattle-based garden writer Val Easton and she was chatting with the editor of *Garden Design*. They needed more pictures of Windcliff for an upcoming feature. Was I interested? I jumped at the opportunity. Dan set the challenge for me, saying there hadn't been a decent shot published of his garden with Mount Rainier, the imposing active volcano that dwarfs the outline of Seattle's skyscrapers, in the background. It's such a prominent feature of the garden and Dan has designed the plantings so that the mountain is

gently revealed. But, as is so often the case with garden photography, the weather just had not cooperated during previous shoots. As it turned out, I had two absolutely stunning mornings, both perfectly calm and clear. It was a physical challenge to capture this stunning garden, as I had to move quickly—often with a ladder—since there's such a short window of opportunity to utilise the soft light before the sun reaches its full intensity. My greatest reward for the shoot was that Dan was happy with the images. I can't hope for more when I am photographing someone's garden, as I appreciate they are such personal spaces. This shoot then led me to photograph Skylands (page 104), the Maine property of Dan's good friend Martha Stewart.

SKYLANDS

Skylands is the beloved historic summer home of Martha Stewart, television personality, writer, businesswoman and one of the most famous names in the world of homemaking and beautiful living. Martha is the third owner of this stunning property, located on Mount Desert Island in Maine. She bought the house, built in 1925 by Duncan Candler for Edsel and Eleanor Ford, in 1997 and refers to Skylands as her favourite place. After visiting with Dan Hinkley during the summer of 2016, I can see why.

You know you are entering somewhere special when you come up the stunning, winding driveway of local crushed pink granite through the mossy evergreen forest to the house. The atmosphere of the garden is strongly felt, but it's also a very subtle space and undoubtedly magical. It's a lasting testament to Danish-born Jens Jensen's naturalistic design laid out in the 1920s for the Fords, as well as Martha's care and sensitivity to the landscape since.

The magnificent main terrace retains its original cracked-ice stone work, and looks out to stunning views of Seal Harbor and the surrounding coniferous forest of pine, spruce and hemlock. Kiwi vines grow up the side of the house and over the western terrace's pergola where Martha entertains. Planters, including her Gertrude Jekyll–style pots, are beautifully arranged. Martha uses *faux bois* (false wood) French concrete furniture both inside and out.

One of my favourite areas of the garden is the Lost Pools, where Martha has restored an ornamental pond with a cracked-ice pattern in homage to Jens Jensen's work. Water features are central to this landscape and many of Jensen's other designs. Several other pools, fountains, natural-looking waterfalls and small streams of running water are scattered around the property and cross some of the paths. The sound of flowing water was intended to give visitors cause to pause and reflect, as well as connect them to the natural beauty of the surroundings.

Wandering Skylands' winding paths subtly lit by garden lights and laid with fresh pine needles, when the woodland was completely quiet and still on a misty wet morning, was definitely a highlight of my career. Coming out of the damp and into the most beautiful house you can imagine, I was greeted by the breakfast of my dreams stunningly set out by Martha in her late 1920s kitchen that has been restored and preserved immaculately, as is every detail in this American treasure.

FERRY COVE

SHERWOOD, MARYLAND

This was the home garden of the late James van Sweden who, with plantsman Wolfgang Oehme, started what would become one of the USA's most respected and influential landscape practices, Oehme van Sweden and Associates. It was one of the first firms to move away from traditional, highly manicured lawns to create more naturalistic landscapes, inspired by the great masters of painting, with mass plantings of perennials and grasses. It is a style that became known as the New American garden.

The minimalistic design of this meadow garden, which was once a farm overlooking Chesapeake Bay in Maryland, looks incredibly natural. Tall native coneflowers (*Rudbeckia maxima*) come right up to the edge of the pool, where a bronze snake sculpture by Raymond Kaskey also acts as a hand-rail. I'm so glad I had the opportunity to meet James while I was photographing his outstanding garden, which disappears so successfully into its surrounding landscape.

FEDERAL TWIST

STOCKTON, NEW JERSEY

This is the garden of James Golden, famed for his excellent gardening blog, *View from Federal Twist*, which he describes as the ramblings of a 'New American' gardener. Although he worked in marketing, James discovered gardening later in life. In the years since, he's immersed himself in the gardening community and created this incredibly expressive and thoughtful garden for himself and his partner, above the Delaware River in New Jersey. In 2006, inspired by the work of both Noel Kingsbury and Piet Oudolf, James felled eighty cedars from his 6000-square-metre (1.5-acre) garden to let in light. He then set about re-creating a prairie, using both native and non-native plants that suited local conditions.

James's style groups plants together that are equal in their competitiveness, allowing nature to take its course—he only intervenes when he sees the need. However, this is by no means a low-maintenance garden. When late winter arrives at the end of January, James cuts and burns the entire prairie, making way for the new season's growth. By mid-May, everything is green again.

The garden is completely stunning—a forever changing and highly seasonal landscape that towers over you as you wander its paths and almost completely hides the house by the end of summer.

James has described his landscape as being 'aesthetic, ornamental, even emotional' and I love the discussion between him and William Martin, the creator of Wigandia, on James's blog, about gardens being places for the mind.

WAVEHILL

BRONX, NEW YORK

If I hadn't been there and taken these photographs myself I never would have believed that this is a public park in the Bronx, the northernmost of New York City's five boroughs. It's part of a very urban area, yet this is such a relaxed and natural space.

It was once the estate of financier George Perkins, but in 1960 his family gave it to the City of New York and it was opened to the public as a garden and cultural centre. Across its 11 hectares (27 acres), former director of horticulture Marco Polo Stufano, who retired in 2001 after thirty years of service, created a huge series of garden rooms. I love that part of the garden's mission today is to 'explore human connections to the natural world through programs in horticulture, education and the arts'.

James Golden from Federal Twist told me about Wave Hill, so I made sure to visit on my autumn east coast trip. I particularly loved the Wild Garden, which sits at the highest point of the estate and was inspired by William Robinson's informally planted English gardens (see Gravetye Manor on page 216). At sunset, it really captured my imagination. There's a beautiful old sumac tree and undulating layers of planting with so much detail in them. Plus, at that time of day, the views across the Hudson River and Palisades, south to Manhattan, are stunning.

SAN JUAN ISLANDS

SAN JUAN ISLANDS, WASHINGTON

It was the view across the Haro Strait to Vancouver Island and the Olympic Mountains that originally attracted Edgar and Polly Stern to this stunning piece of land on Washington State's San Juan Island in 1986.

The couple, both now deceased, commissioned architect David Finholm to design their dream home on the heavily wooded site, with famous landscape architect Richard Haag joining the project soon after. Richard, renowned for his work on Gas Works Park in Seattle, had a huge influence on not only the creation of the garden but of the house as well. To him it was imperative that as much as possible of the natural setting should be saved. To ensure this happened, the pair came up with a design breaking up the homestead into smaller structures that could be tucked among the trees and slightly raised so as to protect the trees' roots and the hydrology of the site. This sensitivity is why the garden sits so well within its landscape.

I love the subtlety of this garden and how it is not overly manicured. There aren't a lot of flowers and Richard has worked with the established Douglas firs, adding low-growing plants—shrubs, ferns, perennials, groundcover—to create layers of interest. He also established what he refers to as 'nookeries'—places where the Sterns could take a cup of coffee or a drink and enjoy the vistas— at different points on the property.

While I was there, I ventured off early in the morning to take a photograph of Peter Busby's sculpture of the whale flukes and the view towards the Olympic Mountains, and looked down in the ocean to see a couple of whales breeching. It reminded me how lucky I am to be able to do this work and experience such beautiful moments.

ROHDIE

CATSKILL MOUNTAINS,
NEW YORK

Talented garden designer Dean Riddle and owner
Barbara Rohdie have been working together for
more than a decade to create this lush garden in
New York's Catskills. My timing was perfect for this
one—when I arrived at the beginning of August, the
garden was at its peak. Dean has planted many native
species, but has also selected plants from other
regions of the world with similar growing environ-
ments. This densely packed planting is reflective of
his desire to imitate natural habitats and requires
relatively minimal maintenance or additional watering
now that it is established. I loved the combination of
the exuberant perennial planting, including *Echinacea
angustifolia* and *Rudbeckia triloba* 'Prairie Glow' set
against the clipped box balls and river birch (*Betula
nigra* 'Dura-heat').

LOTUSLAND

MONTECITO, SANTA BARBARA,
CALIFORNIA

For just a short time, I had this garden all to myself and it is one of the favourite moments of my career as a photographer so far. Having early mist blanket the property isn't unusual, since it's located in Montecito, near Santa Barbara on the Californian coastline. On this particular morning the mist lasted for about an hour before clearing. It was completely quiet and the presence of the fog made the atmosphere quite otherworldly.

Opera singer and socialite Ganna Walska (who preferred to be called Madame throughout her life) bought the property in 1941 and worked on the garden for the next four decades. Born in Poland in the late 1800s, she married a Russian count while still a teenager, then during her lifetime had five more husbands. It was during her final marriage to the yogi Theos Bernard that she made the move to California. When the couple divorced, she devoted herself and her substantial wealth to her plants and garden. She even transformed an old swimming pool into a lotus pond, where, each September, a pink hybrid waterlily called *Nymphae* 'Madame Ganna Walska' blooms.

As you wander around the 15-hectare (37-acre) gardens, there's so much to see. There are about twenty-five separate areas, including a blue garden, where she nurtured plants that have silver and blue-grey foliage, and a cactus garden with more than 300 different species grouped by their country of origin. Walska had

an incredible eye for the use of succulents and cacti. You'll notice plants hanging from the trees so they resemble jellyfish and stone figures dotted around the theatre garden. Many of her designs incorporate almost architectural layers: tall stands of trees and palms towering over plantings of groundcovers. She used materials very differently, too—around the lotus pond you'll see borders of abalone shells, and big clam-shells create a fountain.

When Ganna Walska died in 1984, Lotusland became a botanic garden and was opened to the public nine years later. It only came to my attention when a Californian garden designer, Kate Frey, recommended I visit. It's easy to see why Chelsea Flower Show judge Christopher Bailes names it as one of his ten favourite gardens in the world. The morning I spent in solitude here, capturing the details of Madame Walska's creation, will be a memory that stays with me forever.

MANDIN

While the situation of this garden in northern California, with views of San Francisco Bay on one side and the mountains on the other, is unique, it presented designer Brandon Tyson with some difficulties. The climate is extreme and very dry for much of the year, but his design utilised his gift for dramatic elements to great effect. His skilled use of architectural plants and eye for the placement of garden features can be seen in one of my favourite scenes. Here a stepping stone path leads through a gravelled area planted with spiky *Yucca rostrata*, while small egg-shaped stones are scattered between carved-stone water jars. A dead oak tree becomes an almost bonsai-like sculpture behind. This scene is further enhanced by the irregularly sized clipped box balls seen in the distance. I also love the view on the other side of the garden, which is the perfect spot to catch the sunrise from the redwood deck.

At about one hectare (2.5 acres), this is quite a big space and, at times, when you're walking beneath towering palms underplanted with agave, it can feel as though you're in an exotic botanical garden. It's a stunning example of how gardens need time to mature and show their full personalities, as Brandon would say. He has been working here with his client for nearly thirty years.

CEVAN FORRISTT

It's hard to believe you're in San Jose, sitting in Cevan Forristt's home garden. He likes to create a 'private country' for his clients and he's certainly done that for himself; as soon as you step on to the stone paths here, it's as if a part of Asia has come to the suburbs.

Cevan is one of the most interesting designers I've met and fun to be around. When I visited, he was just back from a trip to Iran and full of exciting stories about how he'd immersed himself in the local community and culture there. Cevan's design is inspired by his extensive travels, mostly through Asia, and also his background in stage-set design. He loves to combine Asian artefacts and architectural finds, often with contemporary concrete installations. Planting is more of a subsidiary element, with the focus on drought-tolerant natives and exotics.

His home garden is a very peaceful and relaxed space, and Cevan tends to wander around in bare feet. I found myself following his lead while I was exploring and taking photographs.

One of the interesting aspects about photographing gardens is approaching them. Often, as you're driving down the street, you'll notice a change in the plantings, sometimes on the footpath and in neighbours' gardens, which is a fairly good indication you've arrived before you see the garden you are actually visiting. Gardeners often like to extend themselves beyond their boundary. It was slightly different when I went to visit Cevan—it wasn't a change in the foliage, but piles of ancient stones on front lawns that neighbours were holding for him that gave him away.

Cevan loves to cook for people and entertain in his backyard. I enjoyed an eye-watering but delicious meal there with him and Berkeley artist and gardener Marcia Donahue after photographing. I later read Cevan changed his name because he thought that, if you had an interesting name, you would have an interesting life. It was a joy to meet Cevan and I loved the unconventional and highly expressive home and garden he has created for himself, which was as beautiful and atmospheric inside as out.

HERONSWOOD

KINGSTON, WASHINGTON

Heronswood, in Kingston, Washington, is the famous first garden of world-renowned plantsman, author, plant collector and lecturer Dan Hinkley, before he left for Windcliff (see page 98). For two decades from 1987, Dan and his husband, Robert Jones, created this stunning garden full of rare and unusual perennials, trees, shrubs and vines. The attached nursery featured plants collected by Dan in the wild during his adventures to Asia, Central and South America, New Zealand and Australia.

In 2000 they sold the property, and it was later abandoned, becoming completely neglected over the course of six years. Its revival began when the Port Gamble S'Klallam Tribe bought the property in 2012. Initially the tribe thought it would make a good wedding venue, but with time the landscape revealed itself and many of its rare plants were recovered. Today the garden is a huge success story, and great pride is taken in its management, restoration and advancement as a garden of significance. Dan is now a director at the garden, and with his original passion for plants, he is involved with its new exciting direction as a centre of horticultural excellence and diversity.

I loved the new perennial plantings, which were so beautiful and clever, and my timing was perfect for the iris and agapanthus border that was stunning against the backdrop of redwoods. Wandering the paths in the woodland garden felt like discovering a lost Eden, only made more magical with the morning mist. It was an absolute privilege to spend a few days here capturing this important garden for *Garden Design* magazine.

COOS BAY

COOS BAY, OREGON

In 2016, I photographed a series of gardens that had been created by Buell Steelman and Rebecca Sams for *Garden Design* magazine. They're the husband and wife team who have run Mosaic Gardens in Eugene, Oregon, since 2002. They work fantastically together, not only designing the gardens as a duo, but maintaining them as well.

This property is located on the water and has some amazing views, but for me the interest lies in the garden. Buell and Rebecca use mass plantings of species so effectively, creating a stunning tapestry of colour and texture regardless of the angle from which they are viewed. Many of the plants are kept low to avoid damage from the strong winds that hit the coastline. It's quite a contrast to the towering redwoods that surround the garden, as they so

often do in the Pacific Northwest. The couple also had to take into account the local deer population, which tends to make short work of a lot of gardens in the area, and used plants they don't like to eat. The family who lives here also has children, so Buell and Rebecca have ensured there are a couple of lawns and a meadow for the family to have usable space.

I photographed at sunset and first thing in the morning, and my favourite images were taken as the rising sun backlit the Japanese maple trees and the entire mosaic of planting in the ornamental garden that surrounded them. It's such a balanced and beautiful planting scheme, and this garden, like their others, really shows Buell and Rebecca's skill in design, attention to detail and high standards of maintenance.

IN SITU

REDDING, CONNECTICUT

This stunning three-hectare (7.5-acre) sculpture garden in Redding, Connecticut, is a decade-long collaboration between Seattle-based landscape architect Richard Hartlage from Land Morphology and art collector and owner Mike Marocco. It's a garden on a grand scale, with soft, romantic mass plantings of grasses and perennials set against structures and contemporary art. One of the more interactive pieces is Danish artist Jeppe Hein's *3-Semicircular Mirror Labyrinth*, consisting of a number of mirrored pillars that reflect both the viewer and the view, including the black mondo grass planted around it. A water feature, called the *Gathering*, is set in the midst of a field of black-eyed susans.

The garden consists of eighteen different rooms, including a 6000-square-metre (1.5-acre) meadow and terraces. Each area is subtly connected to the next by grass, stone and woodland walks with stepping stones. I love the way the garden areas are more formal closer to the house then, as you venture further, they become looser in feel, with bold sweeps of colour that are beautifully highlighted by the morning sun. Particularly beautiful during autumn, the garden is enhanced by the surrounding deciduous woodland of the Saugatuck Waterfall Natural Area.

THE STUMPERY

VASHON ISLAND, WASHINGTON

In 2006, when Pat and Walter Riehl bought their property on Vashon Island, a twenty-minute ferry ride across the Puget Sound from Seattle, they uncovered, in native woodland behind the house, a shaded ravine hidden by weeds. This immediately sparked an idea in Pat, who'd attended a European tour with British fern expert Martin Rickard that had taken them to view ferneries and stumperies, including one at Highgrove, the Prince of Wales' property in the UK. This style of garden was popular in the Victorian era and the first notable one was created in 1856 at Biddulph Grange in Staffordshire. Inspired by these stumperies, she commissioned Martin to work with them to design and plant one in the ravine.

The result, the largest stumpery in the United States, is meticulously maintained by Pat and is nothing short of magical. As you access the garden through the pergola, which is piled high with stumps on all sides, you enter another world. Around 175 native madrone and Douglas fir stumps were collected and placed in the garden. As they slowly decompose, these stumps act as sculptural interest and become home to a multitude of plants. Colour is kept to a minimum, with only shades of green and brown. The only flowers here are *Epimedium* in the form of groundcover. This restraint only adds to the peaceful nature of this beautiful and well-crafted space, which is expertly planted with a huge diversity of rare and unusual ferns. Moss is allowed to enter and softens the garden naturally and Pat's pride and joy are the south-eastern Australian tree ferns, *Dicksonia antarctica*.

PFEIFFER GARDEN

VASHON ISLAND, WASHINGTON

Garden designer David Pfeiffer's home is on Vashon Island, just across the water from Seattle, with enviable views of Puget Sound. The story of his garden is an interesting one and reveals the progression of a garden designer's style.

David used to have a much more complicated and high-maintenance garden with intricate planting, but decided to simplify it since, during the past few years, he's refined his style and become much more minimalistic. His strong design and new aesthetic has also freed up his time, so he can now enjoy his garden more during time off.

David is known for combining the disciplines of horticulture, landscape design and interior design so that inside areas transition seamlessly to those outside. You can see this in his home garden, where there are several outdoor entertaining areas that beckon you in this highly usable and beautiful garden.

There's a stunning seating area beneath grapevines covering a pergola above the pool. I captured it with the long shadows created when the sun was dropping in the sky. That time of day was also perfect for photographing David's labyrinth where he goes in the mornings to meditate.

David beautifully contrasts the sharp edges of hardscaping around the pool and pergola area with loose perennial plantings and a meadow area, which extends to the new mounding created around the pool. The garden transitions sensitively into the surrounding landscape with no distinct edges, instead becoming slightly wilder and less defined as you move further from the house.

My favourite scene was captured during the golden hour of sunset, which seems to linger so beautifully during the Pacific Northwest summer. I loved the defined lines of the pool, contrasting with *Imperata cylindrica* 'Rubra' (Japanese blood grass), *Verbena bonariensis* and the towering redwoods behind. The Pacific Northwest has become one of my most enjoyable destinations to photograph in recent years. The combination of the stunning natural landscape, together with its incredibly good growing conditions and abundance of talented gardeners and designers, who could not be more hospitable, make it one of the richest garden regions of the world.

CADY'S FALLS

MORRISVILLE, VERMONT

This garden in Vermont isn't at all well known, but it is a gem. It actually surrounds a nursery of the same name owned by Don and Lela Avery, where they specialise in and propagate hard-to-find and rare plants, including dwarf conifer, alpines, bog plants, cacti, lady slippers and rock ferns. But after thirty-seven years, 2017 will be the last year they will sell plants on a regular basis, so I'm glad I visited when I did, at the recommendation of renowned garden designer and preserver Bill Noble.

One of the garden's main features is its many maple trees, which, of course, Vermont is famous for, and they were in brilliant colour while I was there. Throughout the garden there are also some amazingly sculptural conifers, including weeping Norway spruce and European larch. The early morning mist lingering in the garden and surrounds made me feel as though I was in some make-believe world created by Don and Lela.

STONE ARCHES
CATSKILL MOUNTAINS, NEW YORK

Mark Veeder's garden in upstate New York definitely has magic to it, and this is why he wanted me to stay on the property over the weekend I photographed it; he thought it would give me an excellent feel for the place. Mark isn't a gardener by profession—he's very entrepreneurial, being creative director at a PR and marketing firm in NYC and also, after the discovery of *Echinacea purpurea* 'Green Envy', the owner of Farmacy Beauty—but during the past twenty-five years has developed an obsession for plants and gardening that has let him create this magnificent weekender.

I love the subtlety and calmness of this garden, which, with its large ponds, integrates so beautifully into the surrounding forest. The property, particularly in the woodland garden, is full of stunning plants that show Mark's love of interesting leaf forms. Inspired by Piet Oudolf's work on the High Line, he's planted a meadow of perennials on a bank he calls the Greenhouse Wilds. Near the greenhouse, he also added a sculptural landform based on the work of artist Richard Serra. But my favourite scene takes in the guesthouse across the pond with the Adirondack-style chair Mark built. When I photographed it, the sun was just coming up and there was a light mist over the reflection of the building in the water. It was such an idyllic, peaceful scene and I can see why Mark meditates here.

RANCHO DIABLO

This dramatic and inspiring cactus garden is the work of the three people who live there, Lucia Howard, Margaret Majua and David Weingarten. David and Lucia run Ace Architects, and Margaret is the plants person of the group. Not surprisingly, when you consider David and Lucia have worked on projects for Disneyland, this is a creative garden with strong architectural shapes and a touch of whimsy.

The property, located near Lafayette just outside of San Francisco, gets its name from Mount Diablo, which the garden overlooks. It's hot and dry here and, with years of drought conditions in California, this is one of the most interesting and well planted dry-climate gardens I've seen, especially on a residential scale.

I love the view out the back door, with the purple gravel path, ponytail palms (*Beaucarnea recurvata*) and the mass planting of cactus with contrasting sizes and forms, including golden barrel cactus (*Echinocactus grusonii*) and monstrose apple cactus (*Cereus peruvianus* 'Monstrosus').

The Recycled Garden below is open and sunny. Its circular lawn features statues from an old San Francisco library, salvaged palm trees and an aloe hedge.

One of my favourite shots is of the terrace—the backlighting of the great columns of cacti and the pods of the wisteria are very beautiful. Here also is an outdoor setting created from horse-shoes. I'm so glad sculptor Marcia Donahue told me I should visit.

KARSEN GARDEN

MARIN COUNTY,
CALIFORNIA

Jeff and Beth Karsen, the original owners of this property just north of San Francisco, are art collectors and wanted to extend their modern, minimalist aesthetic into the garden. They commissioned Brandon Tyson, who had worked with this wild mountainside terrain for more than thirty years. Although Brandon was initially known for utilising a huge diversity of plants, his aesthetic has been refined and really pared back over the years, so that in this garden a fewer number of species are used. The effect, however, is perhaps even more dramatic. I photographed this garden in 2009 and it's still one of my favourites and so unique.

The garden has a Japanese feel to it, with a bold, circular sweeping lawn, bordered by repeated plantings of *Ligustrum japonicum* 'Texanum' (waxleaf privet). Topiaries have been shaped into artistic, modernist forms and planted between golden *Robinia* trees, with a groundcover of *Acorus gramineus* 'Ogon' (golden Japanese rush). One of my favourite walkway and planting combinations is also here, where Brandon has massed clipped box balls and *Acorus gramineus* 'Pusillus Minimus Aureus' beneath *Otatea acuminata aztecorum* (Mexican weeping bamboo), with native Monterey cypress trees behind.

DIGGING DOG

MENDOCINO COAST, CALIFORNIA

This is the home garden of Gary Ratway, a hugely talented garden designer and plantsman, on the north Californian coast near Mendocino. His wife, Deborah Whigham, runs the nursery of the same name on the couple's property. I photographed this garden for *Gardens Illustrated* in 2008; it was my first experience of photographing an American garden and I was completely enchanted. I loved Gary's strong design style, which is influenced by the gardens that resulted from the collaboration between British architect Sir Edwin Lutyens and Gertrude Jekyll. This is contrasted with his loose plantings, set within a forest of enormous redwoods and the rammed-earth house. It was such an atmospheric garden I just had to revisit and try to capture it with the frequent coastal mist that eluded me on my first visit.

I returned in 2016 and loved seeing the changes in the garden, but I was also glad to see my favourite areas still there: the gravel pathway, with wooden bench at one end, lined with exuberant plantings of *Verbascum* and *Euphorbia*, with archways clipped though bordering tall hornbeam hedges. It looked particularly romantic on this misty morning.

I also loved seeing the more minimalistic garden at the back of the house, which had been developed further with more hornbeam columns, loosely clipped box balls and lavender planted on mounds. Here, one of the pathways is lined with *Stipa gigantea* and I imagined Gary brushing through these golden grasses as he left his onsite office at the end of each day. The garden had also grown quite significantly on one side, where there were enormous hornbeam columns lining the paths and new and exciting areas of planting, that felt slightly wilder. Digging Dog was every bit as magical as I'd remembered.

SEAN HOGAN

PORTLAND, OREGON

You know you must be getting close to Sean Hogan's home garden in Portland, Oregon, as the streetscape starts to change and all sorts of interesting and exotic trees, including several eucalyptus species, begin appearing. Then, on arrival out the front, you can barely see the house through the dense planting of the most incredible collection of plants that also covers the nature strip (known locally as hellstrips).

Sean's love and knowledge of plants is awe-inspiring, as are his many stories attached to specific plants he's discovered in the wild. He first became hooked on plant hunting when he was given a guide to cacti as a pre-teen and found two species in the book that were native to his home state. It ignited a passion that consumed family holidays when he was younger and has since seen him travel to South America, South Africa and the western landscapes of the United States and northern Mexico. His Instagram feed is full of these regular plant-hunting trips.

Sean also runs the large and very successful Cistus Nursery on Sauvie Island, renowned for its unique collection of Mediterranean climate, southern hemisphere and hardy tropical plants, among others.

Sean is a hugely talented designer, working with his unique plant palette, including drought-tolerant species, in inspiring landscapes that range from smaller, domestic projects to much larger commercial ones. His home garden, particularly the backyard, is an oasis, and I don't think I have seen neighbours better screened off in an urban setting. Sean loves to entertain and says he actually prefers his garden at night, when a totally different atmosphere takes over and the strong architectural shapes of the leaves can be clearly seen.

GREAT DIXTER

NORTHIAM, RYE, EAST SUSSEX,
ENGLAND

My connection to Great Dixter began when
I heard about it from Juliet Roberts, the long-
standing and much-loved previous editor of
Gardens Illustrated. It was her favourite garden
and she told me I had to visit. Spending a
weekend there in the glorious Arts and Crafts
house and meeting new friends, I began to
understand the significance of this remarkable place, one of the most famous and loved
gardens in England.

Great Dixter was the home of legendary
gardener and garden writer Christopher Lloyd
(1921–2006), who lived here most of his life
and spent almost fifty years writing about it,
producing twenty-five books. Christo, as he was
known, inherited the garden from his parents.
His father Nathanial Lloyd, with architect
Edward Lutyens, laid out the structure of the
garden, including the clipped yew hedges and
generous borders that remain today. The planting within though has been Christo's domain,
and he created a legacy of highly innovative and
creative planting and thinking. Christo famously
stopped mowing the lawns to create a series
of rich wildflower meadows.

In 1992, Christo took on Fergus Garrett as head
gardener and the two worked in tandem until
Christo's death, constantly creating, challenging
and inspiring each other with their new planting
ideas, which are not repeated even when successful. Together they controversially ripped
out the rose garden and replaced this with a
spirited garden full of exotics with a tropical
feel. Chatting with Sean Hogan (see page 174),
it was amazing to hear how he sent Christo his
first hardy banana, *Musa basjoo*, then, not long
after, received a short hand-written letter from
him describing how he'd just torn out the
rose garden.

Great Dixter is a high-maintenance garden,
but feels nothing like that. With its slightly
wild planting and narrow paths, you often have
to push your way through the grasses and
perennials, but this only helps you to feel more
connected to the garden. Fergus has been key to
Dixter's continued success and evolution, carry-
ing on and growing the legacy left by Christo.

BRYAN'S GROUND

PRESTEIGNE, HEREFORDSHIRE,
ENGLAND

Garden photography is all about timing, and
never more so than with this garden, the
work of David Wheeler and Simon Dorrell in
Herefordshire near the border of Wales. At the
end of May, the 20,000 blue iris 'Papillon' flower
in the orchard and lead you all the way to the
back door of the house. I arrived in the evening
and it was raining, but the next day I was excited
to wake to a misty morning. I loved the view
along White Poplar Avenue in the arboretum
as the sun filtered through the mist. I could not
have asked for better conditions that spring
morning, which perfectly suited one of the most
romantic gardens I have visited.

Bryan's Ground, established in 1913, maintains its original Arts and Crafts design, but the planting has become softer and wilder since David and Simon moved here in 1993. I tend to favour gardens that have limited hardscaping—for me, gardens are all about the plants and the changing seasons. Here, I love the contrast between the clipped formal hedges, columns and spheres against the wilder planting and self-seeding species. It's a dream garden to walk through, as your eye is led along the mown pathways often towards a beautiful feature or building. There are some stunning views across the neighbouring countryside, too. Simon is also an artist, and I love the way he and David have arranged objects found on the property in such a whimsical and creative way. In one part of the garden, old bikes hung in a tree become sculpture, and in another they have beautifully arranged porcelain fragments in wooden printer trays.

While I was there, David and Simon invited me to have lunch with them beneath the wisteria with my colleague Christine Reid. It was a wonderful way to connect to both the owners and their beautiful garden.

WOOLBEDING

For forty years Stewart Grimshaw and Simon Sainsbury worked to create this magnificent garden. They took over the lease in 1972 when the garden was completely overgrown, although both thought it was magical. They worked with a number of designers, including Lanning Roper (who devised the wide double border leading up to the house) and Isabel and Julian Bannerman, in the coming years to create a series of beautiful, intimate garden rooms. Some, like the herb and fountain gardens, are protected by high walls. Simon died in 2006, but Stewart continues to live on the West Sussex property, which is now in the hands of the National Trust, further developing it.

One of the most prominent features of the garden is its long paths, starting with the one that leads to the house. They often draw the eye towards an interesting fountain, gate or piece of art. In fact, one of the fascinating aspects of this garden is the blend of the traditional in the buildings, plantings and the sharply trimmed hedges and topiary with the contemporary sculptures, like the one by William Pye on the lawn in front of the house.

Further afield on the property that spans 10 hectares (25 acres) are far less formal gardens, including meadows planted with narcissi, crocuses and tulips and shaded by almost sculptural, gnarled oriental plane trees. My favourite photograph from this series looks out over a meadow of flowering jonquils and tulips. It took many photographs to get the framing with the fence line and the landscape behind it just right. The light was also beautiful on this early spring morning. I know the light is good when I am actually running around a garden, following its first rays and trying to capture this softness, and when it starts to highlight certain features or parts of the garden.

DYFFRYN FERNANT

DINAS, FISHGUARD,
PEMBROKESHIRE, WALES

Visiting Dyffryn Fernant is one of those experiences that encapsulates why I love my work so much. Actually, time spent there didn't even feel like work. The garden is located on ancient land in the Pembrokeshore Preseli uplands, from where the bluestones for Stonehenge were excavated.

I first visited and photographed Dyffryn Fernant in May 2008, and knew the place was special from that moment. Over the years, I've kept in touch with owners Christina Shand and David Allum, and it was a garden I longed to revisit. Noel Kingsbury also had his eye on it and when he suggested I go, I jumped at the chance. There is so much soul and energy there—you can feel it deeply—and this was even more apparent upon my return in September 2015, when I spent a couple of days there staying in the Long Barn and taking pictures. It's a garden that has deservedly received widespread acclaim as one of the most inspiring in Wales.

When she began developing the 2.5-hectare (6-acre) site more than twenty years ago, Christina was dealing with wilderness on what was previously a sheep farm. Initially she planned only a front and kitchen garden on the difficult, rocky site. There was little topsoil and areas of marsh and bog, but she has responded to the landscape and turned these attributes into features of the garden, so that it is very much of its place. When you stand

in the Magic Garden, a circular wildflower meadow that sits above the house, you cannot see where the garden ends and the surrounding landscape begins.

Christina found inspiration in the writings of Christopher Lloyd and Beth Chatto, so her garden is extremely well planted, with slightly more stylised and intensive areas immediately around the house. The view out her door to the front garden is breathtaking, especially in September when the dahlias and salvias are flowering and the crimson glory vine is turning its autumn hue. Plants that prefer good drainage grow in her Courtyard Garden next to the Long Barn. She's placed pots along the path there, so that the direct route is obscured. There is now also a library she invites visitors to spend time in and read.

As you move further from the house, the garden becomes wilder and even more naturalistic. In the Bog Garden—one of her favourite parts—Christina has largely let nature decide the growth patterns of the community of plants, including *Gunnera*, *Astelia* and *Phormium*. Further afield is Waun Fauch, a Welsh marsh, again left to nature and home to native wildlife and flora. This is a skilfully created garden that comes straight from the heart, is connected to its landscape and is pure joy to visit.

ABERGLASNEY

LLANGATHEN,
CARMARTHENSHIRE, WALES

Aberglasney is a relatively new garden in a sense, having only opened to the public in 1999, but it is one with a long history. Set in the beautiful Tywi Valley, in Carmarthenshire, West Wales, its story stretches back to the Middle Ages, when it was mentioned in a poem. But it is better documented after the mid-1500s when the first of a number of noblemen and clergy bought the property.

The estate was later broken up and fell into a state of complete neglect, both uninhabited and vandalised. Its remarkable restoration began in 1995, when American benefactor Frank Cabot provided the money to the Aberglasney Restoration Trust to buy the rundown house and gardens. The rehabilitation was documented in the BBC program, *A Garden Lost in Time*. Since then the garden has developed immeasurably, and was the only Welsh garden to make the UK Royal Horticultural Society's list of top ten formal gardens to visit in 2015.

Head gardener Joseph Atkin was appointed in 2011 and has been instrumental in pushing the garden forward with its new direction, and it has perhaps never looked better. At the centre of its four hectares (10 acres) is a unique Elizabethan cloister garden, as well as newer areas including a Jubilee Woodland and stunning circular Upper Walled Garden, designed by Penelope Hobhouse.

HINDRINGHAM HALL

HINDRINGHAM, NORFOLK, ENGLAND

This dreamy, romantic garden in Norfolk dates back to 1100 AD and is surrounded by one of the only complete moats left in this part of England. These images were published in *Gardens Illustrated* and I was so pleased the cover featured my favourite scene of the sun coming up over the house with a breath of mist rising from the surface of the medieval moat. This photograph was taken on my second visit here, and it took a total of sixteen hours of driving to get the exact light I needed for this shoot to work. More and more, as with most things, I realise photography is often about effort and how far you are prepared to go. I know I have been to just about the ends of the world, especially in the beginning, when I gave this career everything I had to succeed.

The current owners, Lynda and Charles Tucker, have been working on this garden for more than twenty-two years and they open to the public twice a week in summer. They have created a peaceful garden, with a lovely balance between formal and informal. Closer to the house is the more manicured Formal Garden with lawns, bordered on three sides by herbaceous borders, and the pergola with scented clematis and roses. These formal areas contrast beautifully with the wilder areas, like the Bog and Wild gardens. I loved the narrow winding paths in the Water Garden, as the sunlight filtered through the trees and over the bridge, highlighting the dense planting of primula, hellebores, hosta and day lilies.

LONG BARN

SEVENOAKS WEALD, KENT, ENGLAND

Hers is one of the most famous names in the British gardening world, but before Vita Sackville-West went to Sissinghurst she lived here in Kent. Vita and her husband Harold Nicolson bought the fourteenth-century house in 1915 and spent the next fifteen years developing the style they would take to Sissinghurst. They moved the long barn, for which the property is named, up the hill to the existing house and turned it into a sitting room.

Vita's characteristic romantic and exuberant style has been beautifully maintained and enhanced by current owners, Rebecca and Lars Lemonius, who bought the property in 2007.

Like Sissinghurst, Long Barn consists of many different garden rooms, arranged here in a terrace fashion down a gently sloping hill. As is the case with many of the best British gardens, the old house also offers a beautiful backdrop. I love the photograph of the view taken from the Rose Garden, looking down to the Box Parterre and Main Lawn with its distinctive avenue of clipped Irish yews, and into the distant Kentish countryside.

The planting is abundant and soft, with largely pink and grey tones. There are stepping-stone paths through the trees and across meadows that have been left to grow with wildflowers. Rebecca and Lars have succeeded in creating a loose and natural feel to the planting, enhanced by self-seeding.

GELLI UCHAF

RHYDCYMERAU, LLANDEILO,
CARMARTHENSHIRE, WALES

Gelli Uchaf means 'the upper little grove', and
this enchanting garden has a dreamy setting
800 metres (2625 feet) above sea level with
views to lush, rolling countryside that surrounds it. It is, however, a challenging, steep
site, with extremely high rainfall and cold
winters. Gardeners Julian and Fiona Wormald
bought the property, located near Llanybydder
in Carmarthenshire, over twenty years ago and
have been working together on the garden and
developing their style ever since. It's a small
garden of about 5000 square metres (1.2 acres),
planted around their seventeenth-century
Welsh longhouse and part of a larger property
incorporating 2.5 hectares (6 acres) of rich
wildflower meadows. I loved climbing up to the
top of these at sunrise, and taking in the view of
this serene setting.

Julian and Fiona currently use a naturalistic,
intermingling style of planting, consisting of
many layers of perennials, bulbs and shrubs.
They also use native species, since their particular interest is in providing habitats for insects
and invertebrates. I could see the inspiration
a visit to Monet's garden in Giverny brought
them, particularly in their terrace garden in
front of the house, which was soft, painterly
and textured. There were so many details in the
planting, including masses of *Aquilegia vulgaris*
(columbines) and *Clematis montana* 'Broughton
Star' that was spilling over the stone walls
when I visited in late May. Julian also writes a
detailed and fascinating blog, called The Garden
Impresssionists, about their experiences.

GRAVETYE MANOR

WEST HOATHLY, SUSSEX,
ENGLAND

It's been said you can tell the quality of a garden by visiting it at the end of summer. When I arrived at Gravetye Manor, an award-winning boutique hotel in Sussex, at the end of August, it was luxuriant and full of colour—I thought it couldn't possibly look any better. Gravetye is considered to be one of the most influential gardens in English gardening history. In 1884 it became the private home of famous Irish gardener and writer William Robinson. He was one of the first people to experiment with relinquishing control and allowing nature to enter the garden. His approach began to gain popularity with the publication of his book *The Wild Garden* in 1881. The financial success of his writing allowed him to buy Gravetye Manor and the 80 hectares (200 acres) of land surrounding it.

After Robinson's death in 1935, the property was left to the Forestry Commission and it fell into disrepair. Then, in the 1950s, it was leased by a restaurateur who began its refurbishment. The famous garden, however, only began to be rejuvenated in 2010, when Jeremy Hosking took ownership. Tom Coward, who worked alongside Fergus Garrett at Great Dixter for three years,

was appointed head gardener in the same year. Jeremy and Tom's goal was to conserve and re-create Robinson's work, as well as continuing to evolve the garden by honouring his experimental style. Much of what you can see in these images has been achieved over the course of about five years.

The feelings a garden evokes as you walk around it are always interesting. Some gardens I connect to more than others. Although this Arts and Crafts manor is now being used as a hotel and there are guests most of the time, Tom has managed to achieve and maintain a beautiful atmosphere to this garden, which feels intimate, quiet and special as you wander along one of its many paths. I loved the way Tom has created private and varied places for guests to sit surrounded by stunning mixed plantings of perennials and annuals. My favourite images are taken at sunrise standing on the azalea bank and looking down to the manor, flower garden, meadow and valley beyond with a hint of mist. It's hard for me to imagine a more beautiful garden and setting than Gravetye.

HOPETOUN HOUSE

QUEENSFERRY, WEST LOTHIAN, SCOTLAND

This would have to be the biggest property I have ever photographed. It is a very large seventeenth-century house on a 2600-hectare (6425-acre) estate enshrouded in beauty and history. The Hope family has lived here since the late 1600s, but there is a distinctly modern air about some parts of the garden. Skye, the Countess of Hopetoun, has been inspired by the more contemporary style of naturalistic planting and she has very ambitiously and passionately designed and transformed what was once the property's walled kitchen garden. It's been a huge success and these images were published in *Gardens Illustrated* with text by Noel Kingsbury. It was such a special experience to stay the night at Hopetoun, see this new and exciting garden and spend some time with Skye, who is so hands-on in her garden.

It was September—early autumn in the northern hemisphere—when I visited. But, as is often the case in Scotland, the weather was incredibly changeable. I'd say weather is my greatest hurdle when photographing gardens, as it completely affects the images I am able to capture. Rain showers and rainbows came and went, but the light that came with the changing conditions was absolutely spectacular. I loved the soft pastel colours and layers of the planting on the terrace, and this was particularly stunning just after rain with the backlighting of the rising sun.

TREMATON CASTLE

SALTASH, CORNWELL, ENGLAND

Since the 1980s, Isabel and Julian Bannerman have been creating dreamy and dramatic gardens with touches of history—probably their most famous project is the stumpery at Highgrove, the home of the Prince of Wales. This is their home garden in Cornwall. It is a spectacular location, and the property features the ruins of a Roman fort, a miniature Norman castle, motte (mound), a bailey with gate-house and a separate Georgian villa where the Bannermans now live. Remains of ancient stone walls create stunning backdrops and perfectly complement the Bannermans' exuberant plant-ing and, as they describe them, 'bold borders full of scent, colour, lustre and panache'.

The Bannermans are a very talented couple and when I visited they'd only been working on the garden for three years. What they had achieved in such a short amount of time was incredible. The detail in the plantings, particularly in the double-banked battlement borders behind the house, where you can see roses, fennels, alliums

and lilies, is quite amazing. I also loved the less formal parts of the garden, particularly at the side of their house, where wildflower meadows were left to grow. I felt they beautifully linked the more intensely planted areas and the distant views of the ancient stone walls of the castle.

When I was there, the towering *Echium pininana* were in full bloom in the Tunnel Border and I was able to catch their beauty when the sun was rising behind them.

You can walk along the mown paths that circle up and around the motte to the 9-metre-high (30-foot) Norman keep, with its surrounding meadow of wildflowers, including cow parsley and thyme. From the top, you can catch the spectacular sunrise views of Plymouth Sound. It's from here, looking over the landscape and down to this impressive property, that you can fully appreciate the magic the Bannermans have created here in this most romantic of garden settings.

CAMBO ESTATE

KINGSBARNS, ST ANDREWS,
SCOTLAND

Attached to a historic hotel and guesthouse on the Fife coast, this one-hectare (2.5-acre), largely walled garden, with its naturalistic planting inspired by the work of Piet Oudolf, is particularly innovative and considered one of the finest in Scotland. Following a visit to Hummelo and a number of German gardens, head gardener Elliot Forsyth has created what looks like fields of flowers—there are just masses of them—planted so that the use of colour looks almost painterly (perhaps it's not surprising, since Elliot's wife is a landscape painter). Winding paths meander through the perennials, and the varying heights and different layers of the plantings allow glimpses of the old house, which was rebuilt in 1881 after the original home burned down during a raucous staff party in 1879.

For me, capturing this garden in its full glory meant getting up before the sun then waiting until the end of the day. It's when the light comes from low in the sky that the use of colour and texture can be seen most clearly, especially with this style of planting.

CHAPELSIDE

MUNGRISDALE, PENRITH, CUMBRIA,
ENGLAND

You can't beat a garden that thrives in such a windswept, wild landscape—it is a harsh but beautiful setting. Even with the high winds and cold winters, the garden at Chapelside, with that backdrop of golden hills, is sensitive and subtle. It's a beautiful collaboration between husband and wife, Robin and Tricia Acland. Robin does a lot of the stonework visible around the property, while Tricia is largely responsible for the plantings. She invokes a very natural style and more recently has chosen to let the plants self-seed—it adds to the gentle nature of this property, which seems to sit so lightly within its landscape. There is subtle artistry there, too. You can see it in the rock wall covered in moss, where Robin has introduced a grid of sticks into a mossy wall.

Robin and Tricia arrived at the property, part of the Lakes District, in 1976. At the time Chapelside was a working farm—its only garden was full of vegetables. But Tricia had become interested in gardening and was looking for a project. The small stream running through the property was a huge attraction for them. They started close to the house, removing walls to give the garden flow, and worked out from there. There wasn't a plan, except that Tricia wanted a garden where there was always something flowering. I loved visiting the garden and spending some time with its creative owners, who so obviously love and nurture it.

LE JARDIN PLUME

AUZOUVIILE SUR RY, NORMANDY, FRANCE

One of the ways I discover gardens is through the connections I make while photographing or visiting other gardens. While I was at Great Dixter (page 178), Aaron Bertelsen, who lives there and works in the vegetable garden, told me this was one of his favourite places, especially during autumn. I travelled to Normandy to see what he meant.

Like all good gardens, when you walk through the gates it's like entering another world. Patrick and Sylvie Quibel bought what was a flat parcel of land that included an orchard—almost three hectares (7 acres) in total—in the French countryside in 1996. Now, there are lots of elements to discover, but the garden is best known for its hedges clipped into sharp yet playful shapes interspersed with naturalistic plantings of grasses and perennials.

There are many parts of this garden with which I fell in love. The pool is a very simple square bordered by several species of *Miscanthus sinensis*. Pathways meander through the property and at times, with the perennial grasses growing high, you are dwarfed by them as you push your way through to the next area. Old buildings around the property provide interesting backdrops for the gardens, particularly when you're taking photographs.

I arrived at Le Jardin Plume in autumn, when the grasses are at their zenith. It's during this time you can see where the garden gets its name from: the French translates to 'The Feather Garden'.

Sometimes taking images of gardens isn't quite as simple as it might seem. I visited Le Jardin Plume several times over a few days, but it was only on the final morning I was able to capture this exquisite light. I found myself on a huge ladder to take the photograph of the orchard with its piles of clippings over the plantings of Yaku Jima Japanese silver grass. One of my favourite images captures the repeated triangular shapes of the clipped beech and hornbeam hedges and boxwood in the Autumn Garden. It can take a lot of shots to capture exactly what the designer was trying to do within your frame, which I was reminded of when I took that particular image.

HUMMELO

GELDERLAND, NETHERLANDS

Piet Oudolf is one of the most famous and influential garden designers working in the world today. A leading figure in the New Perennial movement, characterised by its focus on texture, structure and making the most of a plant's life cycle, Piet is responsible for the planting on the High Line in New York City. Opened in 2009 this groundbreaking and much-loved park was created on a disused rail line. People have responded in an overwhelmingly positive way to Piet's planting, which brings nature and a feeling of the wild to the highly urban Meatpacking District.

This is Piet and his wife Anja's home garden, set in the midst of farmland near Arnhem in the eastern Netherlands. It was a bit of a dream to be there with colleague Noel Kingsbury. Noel, a hugely prolific and influential garden writer, has worked alongside Piet and been central to an increasingly international movement, bringing to the world this new style of naturalistic planting. Piet's work, as Noel states in *Planting: A New Perspective*, 'appeals not only to our love of beauty and a certain sense of order, but also to the high level of diversity and openness to dynamic change that biodiversity needs.' It was incredible to see the much-photographed Hummelo in person, with its one-hectare (2.5 acre) garden either side of the traditional farmhouse. Irregularly shaped, clipped yew hedges border the garden and contrast with Piet's highly innovative planting, which looked amazing in early September. This shoot very much depended on working with light, which luckily delivered on the second morning I visited. I loved shooting into the light, with the morning dew glistening on the transparent grasses. It was then I could appreciate the absolute magic of this garden. It was also the perfect misty morning to use my drone to capture the setting of this iconic garden and reveal its design from a different perspective.

LA FOCE

CHIANCIANO TERME
(SIENA), ITALY

Landscapes were my initial inspiration as I became interested in photography in my mid-twenties. I'd completed a science degree and started travelling the world, but Tuscany was always the romantic landscape I longed to visit and capture. One particular much-photographed winding road lined with cypresses, in the Val d'Orcia, a UNESCO World Heritage Site, caught my imagination, so I set out to find it. When I did it was pure beauty. Years later, it was interesting to revisit this famous road, now that my attentions had turned towards gardens. I discovered it had actually been planted by the owners of La Foce as a vista for them to look upon.

La Foce was the home of an aristocratic Anglo-American writer named Iris Origo. She and her Italian husband, Antonio, bought the rundown estate in 1923. Although drawn to the land-scape, Origo first wrote about it as being 'a lunar landscape pale and inhuman … a land without mercy and without shade'. They employed English landscape architect Cecil Pinsent to

work with them to transform the setting and create what is now considered one of the finest twentieth-century gardens in Italy. They also had a lasting impact on the region, as they restored not only their estate, but surrounding buildings and lands as well.

La Foce is built on a number of levels, where formal terraces are divided into rooms—Fountain, Lemon and Rose gardens, as well as an orangery, are included—bordered by box. I particularly loved the Lower Garden, planted by Cecil in 1939, where double box hedges are clipped into angular shapes. Looking out onto that winding road in the distance, I reflected on the beauty here and how far I'd travelled since first sighting that road.

MILL GARDEN

RASCAFRÍA, MADRID, SPAIN

Landscape designers Miguel Urquijo and Renate Kastner have created a stunning small garden here in Rascafría, at the back of an old mill. It's a very sensitive garden that has been adapted to the landscape, with views out to the Sierra de Madrid in the background. They have carefully selected a small variety of plants that cope with the site's acidic soil and don't overwhelm or compete with the surrounding landscape. The birch trees blend well with the existing distant woodland of oak and ash trees, and contrast beautifully with the dark green foliage of the organic yew hedge that is clipped into irregular shapes. Colour is introduced into the garden with plantings of lilies, heather, iris and *Stachys byzantina* 'Silver Carpet' (lambs' ears).

The low stone wall at the rear of the garden creates a lovely sense of enclosure, but still allows one to see the picture as a whole. The surrounding landscape is particularly beautiful when viewed from the wooden bench at the rear of the garden. Miguel was there clipping right up until I photographed and I loved the way he shaped the yew and heather, which suggests the shapes of the mountains.

FERNANDO MARTOS

GUADALAJARA, MADRID, SPAIN

Fernando Martos is a young landscape designer based in Madrid. In Spain, gardens are often created in the more formal style typical of Italy, but Fernando is quickly being recognised for his talent and innovation. After studying at the School of Landscaping and Gardening in Madrid, he worked as a gardener in Yorkshire and fell in love with the seasonal changes and the English style of gardening. Inspired by Beth Chatto, who utilises drought-resistant plants, he began experimenting at his family's property in the south of Spain.

This stunning garden, created by Fernando for his friends near Guadalajara, central Spain, experiences long, hot, dry summers and freezing winters. He has responded by selecting plants from countries with similar Mediterranean climates, and combined perennials, grasses and shrubs that connect the garden to the wider landscape. It's a wonderful example of right plants, right place. Fernando has achieved his goal of creating a garden that is highly aesthetic, but also has a looser, more naturalistic feel incorporating movement, seasonality and excellent use of colour. It was the perfect sunset garden. Golden light backlit the feathered *Stipa gigantea*, which was a strong contrast to the sculptural shapes of clipped *Escallonia rubra* var. *macrantha* (Chilean gum box). I'm looking forward to keeping an eye on Fernando's work in future.

HERMANNSHOF

WEINHEIM, GERMANY

This may be a public park, but garden writer
Noel Kingsbury introduced me to Hermannshof
in Weinheim, describing it as one of the most
exciting gardens in Europe. The reason is that,
since its inception in 1983, it has been considered one of the most experimental gardens
in the world, acting as a trial garden where its
creators work scientifically and creatively to
develop modern plant use. Over the 2.2-hectare
(5.5 acre) site, director Cassian Schmidt grows
plant communities of mainly hardy perennials
and grasses in a naturalistic, intermingling
style, and assesses their competitiveness under
different conditions, recording the exact amount
of maintenance required. The aim is to produce
highly aesthetic combinations that show a
harmony of form and colour, but that are also
sustainable and low maintenance.

Cassian is internationally recognised for his
skill and innovation. In 1998, he took over from
Urs Walser, who had used naturalistic plantings
throughout the garden and put Hermannshof at
the forefront of the New Perennial movement.
One of Cassian's first changes was to replace
a swathe of lawn with prairie-style plantings
divided into areas reflecting the diversity of
prairie conditions. Today the garden contains
around 2500 different perennials, some new
or rare, planted in different habitats—woodland, pond edge, dry meadow and prairie, for
example—throughout the garden, but grouped
together with plants that originate in places with
similar conditions. I envied a couple I met who
visit the garden every Sunday, and are able to
see all of the seasonal and yearly changes in
this remarkable garden.

FARMHOUSE GARDEN

CONSUEGRA, TOLEDO,
SPAIN

In central Spain, near the city of Toledo, the weather is harsh: in the coldest months of the year, the temperature can drop to ⁻15 °C (5 °F) while in summer it can be as hot as 40 °C (104 °F). When I was there in May—early spring in the northern hemisphere—it reached 37 °C (99 °F). Not that you'd know it looking at these images. Within the walls of this property is a small miracle created by garden designers Miguel Urquijo and Renate Kastner.

In this contemporary garden, plants were chosen to offer a sense of place as well as for their ability to survive extremes of weather. Luckily the walls of the patio area help to protect the plants from the wind and, to some extent, also the cold. It's an extremely success-ful garden, created in a most inhospitable place, full of interest and harmony between colours, textures and movement that have been intro-duced using grasses, such as *Stipa tenuissima* (Mexican feather grass). I loved both the view from within the garden and also from above, which allows you to appreciate the skill of the planting, which includes pink *Erysimum* 'Bowles Mauve', grey *Helichrysum italicum*, yellow *Euphorbia* and two varieties of lavender. The front garden contains slightly subtler colours. The planting here is used to create a sense of enclosure, but isn't so high as to disconnect you from the surrounding landscape.

BERCHIGRANGES

GRANGES-SUR-VOLOGNE,
FRANCE

Berchigranges is the garden Noel Kingsbury, renowned garden writer, researcher, lecturer and teacher, has named 'the most beautiful garden he has ever been to', which is an incredible statement considering the number and quality of gardens he's visited around the world. Of course, then I had to visit and, although I was slightly in between seasons at the end of September, I was also completely captivated by this magical garden and its owners.

Monique and Thierry Dronet have created this wonderland in eastern France, in the Vosges Mountains, and it is their life's work. Thierry bought the land—it had once been a quarry but had been planted with Norway spruce—in the late 1970s and set about transforming it. While searching for plants at a local nursery he met Monique, the plantswoman who ran it, and more than two decades later they are still together and forever working and creating. Each year they make a new addition to their extraordinary garden, which already consists of so many unique, themed rooms. When I visited, the Moss Garden, where they'd worked with students to

collect and place moss collected from nearby, was their most recent creation.

The couple freely admits they never sit in their garden—they can't look at it without a critical eye, but that's why it's so good. Instead they cross the road and sit looking out onto an empty field to finally relax and separate themselves from the garden and their art.

Blue is Monique's favourite colour and this is repeated throughout the garden and also their home, where the couple's whimsy and creativity can also be seen. Thierry builds all the structures and furniture in the garden. You can see his work in a stunning grass-covered bridge that straddles one of the ponds he created when he first arrived here, and the stone walls that enclose the Ladies' Chamber with its aromatic plants, including aniseed and mint.

When I visited, one of my favourite parts of the garden was the Bohemian Meadow, filled with asters and grasses that led the eye to the distant rolling landscape. It's a garden that, thanks to Noel, I'm so glad to have visited.

VLINDERHOF

MAXIMA PARK, UTRECHT, NETHERLANDS

This is a very new garden, part of the much larger Maximapark near Utrecht, and one with a fascinating story. Local resident Marc Kikkert had an idea to have Piet Oudolf design the garden and went about finding the support and funding for it. Piet agreed to become involved and Vlinderhof (the name means 'butterfly garden' in Dutch) was planted—and is still maintained—by volunteers. It is encircled by a loose collection of trees and hedges, and is best viewed from a mound near the entrance where you can see how the local residents love and use the park, while also appreciating its many layers, colours and textures. At the time, this was the only garden, other than the High Line, I'd seen of Piet's and, like only a couple of other gardens before, the impact of its beauty and greatness actually brought tears to my eyes. This is the power of his work and reminds me of a quote by Piet in an interview for *The Wall Street Journal*: 'For me, garden design isn't just about plants, it is about emotion, atmosphere, a sense of contemplation. You try to move people with what you do.'

LAVENDER GARDEN

SALAMANCA, SPAIN

I was introduced to the talented husband-and-wife landscape and design team, Miguel Urquijo and Renate Kastner of Urquijo-Kastner, by my friend, landscape architect Thomas Gooch. He was living and working at Great Dixter when they visited. Each project I finish or contact I make can lead to the next, and I love finding gardens this way.

Spain was a fairly untapped area for new garden designs, so there was even more incentive for me to explore. I spent almost a week with Miguel and Renate and loved the opportunity to get to know them and see several applications of their work. It is very sensitive—they work with local conditions and blend their gardens into the surroundings by representing the forms of nature.

This large garden in the pastures of Salamanca is a stunning example of how they create gardens that are at one with the landscape. The owners wanted lawns, so these have been created but minimised, due to the harsh climate here and the excessive irrigation they would require. The entire design is based on a circular theme, which has the added benefit of assisting with efficient irrigation from the owners' well. A minimal plant palette of drought-tolerant shrubs—mainly *Lavandula angustifolia* (English lavender)—has been clustered in islands surrounded by grass. Shrubs are clipped to echo the surrounds of the rolling hills and holm oaks in the distance. *Iris* 'Jane Phillips' provides seasonal interest, before the mass of purple arrives when the lavender flowers. This image won the European Garden Photography award, in the 2016 International Garden Photographer of the Year competition.

GARDENS BY THE BAY

MARINA GARDENS DRIVE, SINGAPORE

Singapore is rightfully known as a city in a garden, and it's impressive to see a country direct so many resources into greening its urban areas. I had to visit to see its most extravagant and futuristic park, Gardens by the Bay. It was only planted at the end of 2007 and first opened to the public in October 2011, but has quickly become one of Asia's top garden destinations. In three years about 20 million visitors viewed its more than one million plants.

The gardens consist of three distinct water-front gardens: Bay South, Bay East and Bay Central, which is still being developed. Bay South, the largest part of the garden, contains the enormous Flower Dome, Cloud Forest and Supertrees.

The Cloud Forest is an otherworldly place, especially when the misters are turned on every two hours. Inside this giant conservatory is a 35-metre-tall (115-foot) 'mountain' and the world's tallest indoor waterfall. You catch a lift to the top of the mountain, walk down along a spiral path and closely view the lush tropical vegetation normally found high in the mountains.

The Supertree Grove is another remarkable area, where a wonderful perspective of the gardens can be seen from an elevated skywalk that connects three of the Supertrees. Each of these eighteen vertical gardens is between 25 and 50 metres (80 to 160 feet) tall. I decided to visit early one morning to see if I could capture the garden before the crowds arrived. I love the perspective offered by the two people sitting at the base of one of the trees. It's also fun to visit here at night, when they host a twice-nightly light show.

It's a hugely successful project done extremely well and I was so impressed by the diversity and health of plant species. It's definitely an inspiring garden and one to return to as it develops and grows.

SHINJUKU GYOEN

SHINJUKU, TOKYO, JAPAN

Cherry blossoms inspired my first visit to Japan, and it has become a country I will always return to as often as I can. Shinjuku Gyoen is a particularly beautiful public park in the middle of Tokyo that dates back to the Edo period (1603–1867). It's one of the best places to view cherry blossoms, which flower at the beginning of spring around the end of March to early April. The park consists of three gardens—French Formal, Japanese Traditional and English Landscape—the latter surrounded by about 400 cherry blossom trees. It is here the Japanese gather in extraordinary numbers to have a picnic or party to celebrate *hanami*, which literally means 'flower viewing', a traditional custom that rejoices in the transient beauty of these spectacular blossoms.

My spring visit to Japan was followed by an autumn trip a few years later, when Tokyo's peak colours appear. Although I was in love with the cherry blossoms, the intensity, diversity and scale of the autumn colours in Japan soon meant this became my favourite time to visit. I revisited Shinjuku Gyoen and it was breathtaking to see the park in its full autumn glory. In Australia, temperatures are generally not cold enough to produce such vivid colours during the changing of the leaves, so it's become a season during which I love to travel to Japan. The traditional Japanese garden was particularly beautiful at sunset (page 286). However, I wasn't the only one capturing the view over the lake of the setting sun backlighting the Japanese maple trees with their canopy of red and gold.

KENROKUEN
KANAZAWA, JAPAN

Like many people at the beginning of their careers, I felt as though I needed to do something to make my work stand out. For years I had dreamed of visiting Japan during the cherry blossom season and thought that the beauty would both inspire me and allow me to expand my portfolio of images. I began researching my first trip online, and found Kenrokuen. Located in Kanazawa and dating back to the Edo period in the seventeenth century, it is considered one of the three most beautiful landscape gardens in Japan. The name Kenrokuen means 'Garden of the Six Sublimities', a title that refers to spaciousness, seclusion, artifice, antiquity, abundant water and panoramic views. According to Chinese landscape theory, these constitute the key attributes of a perfect garden.

When I visited during spring, I couldn't believe that it started to snow. The whole garden took on a magical atmosphere, as though I was in a painting. I saw what I thought was a beautiful composition of a bridge with clipped azaleas and cherry blossom trees and framed this. Then a couple with brightly coloured umbrellas stepped into my frame and crossed the bridge in the snow. I took two images and their placement in one of them perfectly completed the scene. This picture (see page 290) won me the inaugural International Garden Photographer of the Year competition in 2008 and is still one of my favourite images.

NANZEN-IN TEMPLE

SAKYO-KU, KYOTO, JAPAN

This sub-temple at Nanzenji, one of the most important Zen Buddhist temples in Japan, is located at the base of Kyoto's Higashiyama Mountains. It was created in the late Kamakura period (1185–1333) in the *Chisen kaiyu shiki teien* or 'pond strolling' style. It's a highly atmospheric, intimate garden, made even more so by the surrounding forest and a recent downpour of rain that brought out the lushness of the moss and intensity of the Japanese maples in autumn.

GIO-JI TEMPLE
ARASHIYAMA, KYOTO, JAPAN

Gio-ji Temple dates back to the twelfth century and is particularly beautiful to visit during autumn. Located in the Arashiyama district of western Kyoto, this small, peaceful, mossy garden is nestled within a forest and is a stunning sight when viewed through the maple trees while looking back to the thatched roof of the main hall.

ADACHI MUSEUM OF ART

YASUGI, SHIMANE, JAPAN

The Adachi Museum of Art is surrounded by one of the most recognisable modern gardens in Japan. Located near the city of Matsue in the Shimane Prefecture, it takes several hours on a *Shinkansen* or bullet train from Kyoto to reach it.

The museum and garden were created by businessman and art collector Adachi Zenko in 1980, when he was seventy-one years old. Adachi's greatest hope, apart from showing gratitude to his home town, was that visitors would simply be 'moved by beauty'. He felt a strong resonance between Japanese-style gardens and the paintings of his favourite artist, Yokoyama Taikan. Adachi hoped that through the garden's seasonal changes and natural beauty, visitors would be inspired to view the paintings of Taikan with new eyes, appreciate the works of other Japanese painters and, as a result, be touched by beauty. Today, the Adachi Museum of Art gardens are referred to as a 'living Japanese painting'.

Apart from the Juryu-an Garden around the tea house, the other five gardens—the Dry Landscape, White Gravel and Pine, Moss, Pond and Kikaku Waterfall—are all viewing gardens to be contemplated rather than physically experienced. The Dry Landscape garden, which is the main one, maintains a beautiful balance between the surrounding mountain landscape and the garden. Three upright rocks represent mountains, and the white gravel represents the water that runs down from them. The 15-metre (50-foot) Kikaku waterfall in the background is artificial and based on the works of Taikan's painting *Waterfall in Nachi*. It's a garden I have wanted to visit since my first trip to Japan, and I'm glad to have finally seen it and learned about what inspired this great work of art. For me, beauty—capturing and sharing it—is the central inspiration for my work.

LIST OF GARDENS

Stone Arches, p. 160
CATSKILL MOUNTAINS, NEW YORK
Garden owner + designer: Mark Veeder

The Stumpery, p. 150
VASHON ISLAND, WASHINGTON
Garden owner: Pat Riehl
Garden designer: Martin Rickard

Wavehill, p. 116
BRONX, NEW YORK
Current owner: City of New York
Garden designers/previous owners: William
H. Appleton, George Perkins, Albert Millard,
Marco Polo Stufano, John Nally

Windcliff, p. 99
INDIANOLA, WASHINGTON
Garden owner + designer: Dan Hinkley

UNITED KINGDOM

Aberglasney, p. 200
LLANGATHEN, CARMARTHENSHIRE, WALES
Current garden designers and head gardener:
Joseph Atkin, Penelope Hobhouse

Bryan's Ground, p. 185
PRESTEIGNE, HEREFORDSHIRE, ENGLAND
Garden owners + designers: David Wheeler
and Simon Dorrell

Cambo Estate, p. 230
KINGSBARNS, ST ANDREWS, SCOTLAND
Garden owners: Erskine family
Current head gardener: Elliott Forsyth,

Chapelside, p. 234
MUNGRISDALE, PENRITH, CUMBRIA, ENGLAND
Garden owners + designers: Robin and
Tricia Acland

Dyffryn Fernant, p. 194
DINAS, FISHGUARD, PEMBROKESHIRE, WALES
Garden owner + designer: Christina Shand

Gelli Uchaf, p. 212
RHYDCYMERAU, LLANDEILO, CARMARTHENSHIRE, WALES
Garden owners + designers: Julian and
Fiona Wormald

Gravetye Manor, p. 216
WEST HOATHLY, SUSSEX, ENGLAND
Garden designer: William Robinson (late)
Current head gardener: Tom Coward

Great Dixter, p. 178
NORTHIAM, RYE, EAST SUSSEX, ENGLAND
Garden designers: Nathaniel Lloyd (late), Edwin
Lutyens (late), Christopher Lloyd (late), Fergus
Garrett (present)

Hindringham Hall, p. 204
HINDRINGHAM, NORFOLK, ENGLAND
Garden owner + designer: Lynda and
Charles Tucker

Hopetoun House, p. 222
QUEENSFERRY (NEAR EDINBURGH), WEST LOTHIAN,
SCOTLAND
Garden owner + designer: Skye Hopetoun

Long Barn, p. 209
SEVENOAKS WEALD, KENT, ENGLAND
Current owners: Rebecca and Lars Lemonius
Garden designers: Vita Sackville-West and
Harold Nicolson

Trematon Castle, p. 226
SALTASH, CORNWELL, ENGLAND
Garden owners + designers: Julian and Isabel
Bannerman

Woolbeding, p. 190
MIDHURST, WEST SUSSEX, ENGLAND
Current owner: National Trust
Garden owners + designers:
Stewart Grimshaw and his late partner
together with designers, Lanning
Roper, Julian and Isabel Bannerman,
and Simon Sainsbury

EUROPE

Berchigranges, p. 268
GRANGES-SUR-VOLOGNE, FRANCE
Garden owners + designers: Thierry and
Monique Dronet

Farmhouse garden, p. 264
CONSUEGRA, TOLEDO, SPAIN
Garden designers: Urquijo-Kastner,
Miguel Urquijo and Renate Kastner

Fernando Martos, p. 256
GUADALAJARA, MADRID, SPAIN
Garden designer: Fernando Martos

Hermannshof, p. 260
WEINHEIM, GERMANY
Current director: Cassian Schmidt

Hummelo, p. 244
GELDERLAND, NETHERLANDS
Garden owner + designer: Piet Oudolf

La Foce, p. 250
CHIANCIANO TERME , (SIENA), ITALY
Original owners: Iris and Antonio Origo.
Garden designer: Cecil Pinsent

Lavender garden, p. 276
SALAMANCA, SPAIN
Garden designers: Urquijo-Kastner,
Miguel Urquijo and Renate Kastner

Le Jardin Plume, p. 238
AUZOUVIILE SUR RY, NORMANDY, FRANCE
Garden owners + designers: Patrick and
Sylvie Quibel

Mill garden, p. 252
Rascafría, Madrid, Spain
Garden designers: Urquijo-Kastner,
Miguel Urquijo and Renate Kastner

Vlinderhof, p. 274
MAXIMA PARK, UTRECHT, NETHERLANDS
Garden designer: Piet Oudolf

ASIA

Adachi Museum of Art, p. 296
YASUGI, SHIMANE, JAPAN
Creator/founder: Adachi Zenko

Gardens by the Bay, p. 280
MARINA GARDENS DR, SINGAPORE

Gio-ji Temple, p. 294
ARASHIYAMA, KYOTO, JAPAN

Kenrokuen, p. 288
KANAZAWA, JAPAN

Nanzen-in Temple, p. 292
SAKYO-KU, KYOTO, JAPAN

Shinjuku Gyoen, p. 284
SHINJUKU, TOKYO, JAPAN

304

Claire Takacs is an Australian photographer whose passion is photographing gardens and landscapes. She divides her time between Australia, Europe and the USA. Beauty and nature are her inspiration.

Claire's work features regularly in magazines that include *Gardens Illustrated* and *Garden Design*. She has contributed to several books, including *The Gardener's Garden*. She won the inaugural International Garden Photographer of the Year Award in 2008 and every year continues to be recognised for her work.

Acknowledgements

Thanks to my parents, Karl and Lyndsay Takacs, who have provided unconditional love and support. Thank you for allowing me the privilege to follow my dreams and find work that I love, which both connects me to the world and provides freedom.

Thanks to Cloudehill and to Jeremy and Valerie Francis. Thank you for creating and sharing such a beautiful garden, that was so inspiring to me and which set me off on a path that has steered the course of my life ever since.

Thanks to *Gardens Illustrated*, especially Juliet Roberts and David Grenham. It was my ultimate goal to be published by you. Thank you for such a beautiful and inspiring magazine which is so respected around the world and for being the wonderful people you are to work with. I am forever grateful for all of the connections that have come about through working with you.

A huge thank you to Noel Kingsbury, who I've worked with on many of the gardens here. I greatly respect your work and all that you do for the gardening world. It's been an amazing privilege and pleasure to work with you and get to know you over the years. I always know when you send me somewhere that it's going to be special.

Thanks to Christine Reid. I'm so glad Cloudehill connected us. Thank you for so many years of such great collaboration and brilliant writing. It's been wonderful working with you. Thanks also to all the other hugely talented writers I have the pleasure of working with including Tovah Martin, Val Easton, Dennis Schrader, Hilary Burden and Tim Richardson.

Thanks to every single garden owner and designer that has ever opened their world to me. I know these are very personal spaces and I hope I have done some sort of justice in capturing what you have created. I know, though, that it is only ever a small window I get to see in a constantly evolving and much bigger picture. Thank you for all of the hospitality, the meals shared and places to stay. My time spent getting to know you makes my work and life so much richer.

Thanks also to all of the wonderful people in the gardening world who have generously shared their connections with me. I love finding work this way.

Special thanks to garden designers and owners Brandon Tyson, Nancy Goldman, Christina Shand, Dan Hinkley, Jill Simpson, Sally Johannsohn, Sarah Ryan, James Golden, Sean Hogan, Miguel Urquijo, Janet Blair, Martha Stewart, Phillip Johnson and at Great Dixter: Aaron Bertelsen, Fergus Garrett and Thomas Gooch.

Thanks to family friends Ann and Graham Griggs and Hilary Perkins in the UK, who have generously given me a much appreciated and needed home away from home as I have lived a nomadic existence between the hemispheres. Your support and friendship makes the world of difference to me.

Thanks to the magazines that have supported me over the years. I am very grateful to work with you, especially Thad Orr from *Garden Design*, Liz Wilson from *House and Garden*, Victoria Carey from *Country Style* and *Morning Calm*.

Thank you to Pam Brewster from Hardie Grant, for making contact, proposing this book and for your belief in my work.

Published in 2017 by Hardie Grant Books, an imprint of Hardie Grant Publishing

Hardie Grant Books (Melbourne)
Building 1, 658 Church Street
Richmond, Victoria 3121

Hardie Grant Books (London)
5th & 6th Floors
52–54 Southwark Street
London SE1 1UN

hardiegrantbooks.com

All rights reserved. No part of this publication may be reproduced, stored in a retrieval system or transmitted in any form by any means, electronic, mechanical, photocopying, recording or otherwise, without the prior written permission of the publishers and copyright holders.

The moral rights of the author have been asserted.

Copyright © Claire Takacs 2017

A Cataloguing-in-Publication entry is available from the catalogue of the National Library of Australia at www.nla.gov.au

Dreamscapes
ISBN: 978 17437 9352 7

Publisher: Pam Brewster
Designers: Pfisterer + Freeman
Colour reproduction by Splitting Image Colour Studio
Printed in China by 1010 Printing International Limited